ECONOMIC DEVELOPMENT
Evolution or Revolution?

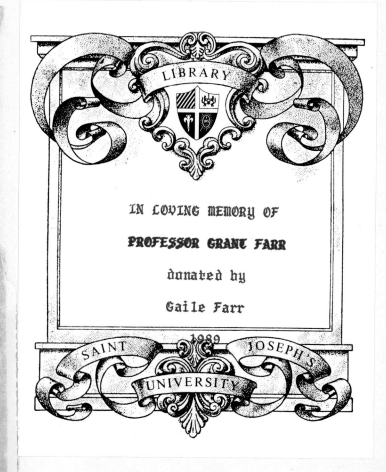

ECONOMIC DEVELOPMENT
Evolution or Revolution?

Edited with Introductions by
LAURA RANDALL
QUEENS COLLEGE

D. C. HEATH AND COMPANY · BOSTON

CONTENTS

INTRODUCTION

The fable of King Midas tells us that man cannot live by gold alone. Nor does gold alone insure economic development: in the Golden Age, Spain had more of the precious metal than any other European power, but spent her treasure on foreign goods. Spanish workmen found that their produce could not compete with imports; as a result, Spanish industries and cities shrank, the knowledge of skilled crafts declined, and Spain became more backward economically than she had been before the Conquistadores set foot in the New World.

Despite the history of the Spanish retrogression, most underdeveloped countries would like a modern Midas to give them the gold or dollars needed to import industrial goods. Unfortunately, it is probably reasonable to assume that neither aid, trade, nor foreign investment will provide the major share of capital required to finance economic development: underdeveloped countries must finance development out of their own resources. The most apparent questions are: (1) Who, within a country, is to foot the bill? (2) How can the funds obtained be directed toward development activities? (3) Could economic development take place more rapidly if the social order were changed? (4) What are the advantages and disadvantages of the *status quo* compared with the proposed new order? (5) Are such advantages or disadvantages more important than economic performance? (6) If not, are the costs of the proposed change so great as to make such a change inadvisable? The ways in which these questions are answered largely depend on whether it is believed that the distribution of political power within a society determines the kind of economic activity that can be carried out, or whether it is thought that the level of economic development is crucial in determining the kinds of political arrangements that can be established. If political considerations are most important in determining the ways in which a country grows, then scholars and demagogues alike say that there is an overwhelming moral case to be made out for a rapid and bloody end to outrageous oppressors; that the old ruling elite, by taking as much income for itself as possible, prevents the rest of society from producing at the highest possible level; and, *that revolution is therefore necessary to restore justice, to break the hold of the traditional power elite, to be able to tax, to be able to create a modern economy.* On the other hand, if underlying economic structure determines the kind of society it is possible to form, *then gradual, evolutionary, largely technical changes are sufficient to ensure economic development, and, along with it, the good life.*

The choice between evolution and revolution as a technique of economic development largely hinges on whether we think that economic or political factors are more important. Marx, for example, was better as an analyst of changes in social structure than as an analyst of economic processes. An ironic result is that Marxist economists stress the importance of political factors in economic development. Capitalist economists stress the importance of technical changes which must be carried out in the process of economic development, regardless of whether the process is violent or relatively peaceful.

The choice between economic development by evolution or by revolution is made difficult by the use of the term "revolution" in several different senses. "Revolution" used to refer to palace coups, in which one faction overthrew the governing clique, but did not establish any important changes in the social order. "Revolution" is now used to indicate violent social upheavals, whether against foreigners or against the local ruling classes. Revolutions directed mainly against foreigners are usually anti-colonial independence movements, but not all independence movements are revolutionary. For example, the Ghanians rather peacefully rid themselves of formal British control, with only moderate changes in local society, while the Americans required a revolution to achieve the same ends. Thoroughgoing domestic revolutions, in which action against foreign interests was trivial, are best exemplified by the French and the Russian revolutions, in which violent changes in social structure were maintained by tyranny. Thoroughgoing domestic revolutions accompanied by actions against foreigners are called nationalist revolutions; in nationalist revolutions, a violent take-over of political power is accompanied by redistribution of property rights from one group within a country to another; to the extent that foreign businessmen are identified with the old régime, they will tend to lose their property, just as property is lost by local supporters of the losing side.

Mexico, Bolivia, and Egypt have experienced bloody and violent nationalist revolutions which nonetheless avoided the extremes of terror and repression that have characterized the communist revolutions in Russia and China. The Cuban revolution is of particular interest, because while in content it resembles nationalist revolutions, in rhetoric it has recently borrowed the language of communist revolutions. The result has gratified the Cuban sense of uniqueness by making the Island revolution fascinating to study, but difficult to categorize.

In discussing the choice between economic development by evolution or by revolution, most of the authors represented in this volume use the term "revolution" in the nationalist sense. For this reason, no explicit discussion of African countries is presented: their problems are still largely centered on the transition from colonial to independent status; as the newly-independent African countries grow, and increase their economic self-sufficiency, changes in the local power structure, and, with them, nationalist revolutions, will become increasingly important.

In discussing the economic and political structure necessary for economic development to take place, a definition of economic development is required. Three characteristics of an underdeveloped country are: (1) that more than one-third of the economically active population is employed in agriculture; (2) that the richest 5 per cent of the population has received more than 30 per cent of the national income in recent years; and, (3) that per capita income is less than 450 dollars. If a country displays any two of these three characteristics, then we regard it as underdeveloped. Thus, Venezuela, which had a per capita income of over 450 dollars, a dominantly agricultural population, and a fairly high concentration of income qualifies as a rich "oligarchic" country rather than as a developed one.

Two underlying changes that are common to the process of economic development emerge from our definition. The first is obvious: as a country changes over from primarily agricultural activity, the addition of mining, industry, or service activities decreases the share of agriculture in gross national product. It is important to note that a decrease in share does not imply a decrease in absolute amount. The second is that together with the change in economic structure, a change in income distribution can be expected. It is frequently argued that since the profits from initial industrialization are so much greater than those that can be obtained from agriculture, the first effect of industrialization will be to increase the concentration of income distribution. As new activities are initiated, and as industrial wage earners begin to form a significant group in society, income distribution tends to become less unequal.

If this equalization of shares does not take place, further economic growth may be impossible, because industrialization requires large domestic markets. Rich people in underdeveloped countries spend a larger share of their income on imports than do poorer people. Therefore, in order to increase the size of the domestic market, income should go to poorer people, who spend their income on domestic goods, rather than to rich people. When an economy is growing, giving a large share of increases in income to poor or middle income groups is politically feasible as well as good economic practice. Two circumstances exist in which such a redistribution — and, with it, rapid economic growth — are extremely difficult to achieve. The first occurs when an economy does not grow faster than is necessary to maintain a constant level of *per capita* income. Then redistribution of income will be opposed by the ruling elites since it will immediately lower their own levels of living. The second exists when individuals or groups in a society are deeply committed to maintaining their relative share of income at all costs.

Perhaps more to the point, when there is small chance of a poor man improving his status in existing society or sharing in any increases in wealth it may generate, the temptation to revolution may become overpowering. In addition to forceful arguments of equity and social justice, it is argued that the short-term costs of revolution will be more than made up for in the long run by the increased ability of the new society to mobilize resources for economic development. Partisans of this line of reasoning argue that under the *status quo* (1) no new project will be undertaken unless the elite owns a controlling share; (2) the experience of Great Britain notwithstanding, the elite cannot be expected to tax or reform itself out of existence; (3) it is entirely possible that under the *status quo,* the income of the elite is maximized. Any change — although benefitting the country as a whole — is to their personal disadvantage. As a result, several of the following steps are necessary: (a) property relations must be restructured as a means of income redistribution because ownership of land and other physical assets is a form of ownership of income. Education is a form of investment in man; a return on this investment takes the form of an increase in earnings that could not be obtained without an education. An important way of equalizing income is therefore making education available to everyone. (b) The state must intervene in domestic trade and foreign commerce to prevent unjust monopoly profits from accruing to the privileged few since size and political bargaining power frequently determine the outcome of economic transactions. (c) Dependence on foreigners — historically linked with "the oligarchy" — must be ended. This entails restrictions on direct foreign investment, the creation of national corporations to operate in key industries, diversification of goods traded and countries traded with, and the formation of a common market within which traditional "imperialists" are denied privileged positions granted to member nations.

Opposed to this line of reasoning are those who find the cost of revolution exorbitant. The short-run effects are bound to be bloodshed, chaos, and lowered income in the cities. Large numbers of technicians and skilled workers who adhered to the old elite will flee abroad; production drops if land reform is involved: until ownership claims are settled, peasants may only produce what they need for their immediate families. If peasants eat more, breeding stock of cattle become traditional "expensive barbecues." Food shortages in the cities will probably be present to some extent for the first few years. Domestic and foreign capital may well be frightened away. If the political tenor of the new régime is unclear, there may be some hesitation about providing foreign aid. And the new government after the revolution may be as unpleasantly vindictive or corrupt as its predecessors.

Since the costs of revolution are great and the outcome uncertain, opponents of revolution argue that while change may be required, it should be undertaken gradually. Economic planning is advocated as the best method of inducing rational change. Ways of convincing existing nations to transform themselves gradually are studied at great length. An understanding of the "decision-making" process assumes paramount importance. It is argued that if only underdeveloped nations understood the American arts of compromise and political procedure, then they would be able to transform themselves into the desired mold. A related statement is that the elite can be scared into change: revolutionaries are necessary; revolution is not.

The readings in this book are designed to present more detailed statements of the various arguments described above, and to provide a survey of the economic results of revolution in several countries. The general case for revolution as the basis of economic development is presented in the first two articles. In the first selection, "Social and Economic Revolution for the Development of Backward Countries," J. E. P. Belshaw states that "the backward countries are now engaged in an attempt to achieve quickly and by direction what Western countries achieved in two hundred years and more through the initiative of countless individuals under free enterprise. Success in this attempt will depend upon drastic changes in the domestic balance of power, upon an internal revolution affecting every detail of the political and social structure, and upon a change in population trends. . . ." His viewpoint is buttressed by a survey of economic and social conditions in underdeveloped countries, which indicates that private enterprise, by itself, cannot bring about rapid economic development. In the absence of effective private enterprise to bring about economic development, Yusif Sayigh argues, the State must take over the role of prime mover in the process of economic development. Nationalist ideology, "guided democracy," and state-run economies take the place of laissez faire and the unseen hand. These arguments are analyzed in the three studies that follow of Bolivia, Brazil, and Mexico.

A detailed examination of the background and initial actions of the nationalist revolution in Bolivia is provided by Professor Carter Goodrich in "Revolution and Economic Development." Pre-revolutionary Bolivia exemplified, more than most countries, the conditions that give force to nationalist ideology: "the economy was characterized by a dangerous reliance on monoproduction, by an archaic system of agriculture, and by a diversion of enterprise and investment into lines that made little contribution to development." Nationalist leaders "insisted that Bolivia could be broken out of the economy of a mining camp only by breaking the power of the great tin companies and that the power of the great landowners had to be broken in order to open the way for the more progressive development of the nation's agricultural resources." Under such conditions, Professor Goodrich argues, it is not only necessary to ask "Can economic progress be advanced by revolution?," but it is also necessary to enquire, "Is economic progress possible by any method other than revolution?"

Concentration of land ownership, monoculture, and lack of industrialization are often the economic basis of revolution. However, a number of countries contain startlingly different conditions. A nation may contain almost neolithic conditions of agriculture and at the same time boast modern industrial installations and transport facilities. A country may contain both a traditional and rigid group of landlords and a growing and powerful middle class. Two factors are crucial in determining whether such a society can transform itself peacefully from a traditional oligarchy to a modern industrial nation: the first is the adaptability of the old elite; the second is the role the middle class adopts: that is, whether the middle class identifies itself with the old elite or with the workers and peasants. If the old elite is intransigent, the likelihood of revolution increases. If the middle class adopts the values of the old elite, then, as it grows richer, it may well turn to investment in land and conspicuous consumption that slows down industrialization. In "Brazil: What Kind of Revolution?," Celso Furtado states that Brazilian society "is an 'open' one to the industrial workers, but not to the peasants." The problem is not one of the values of the rising social group, but rather, of their ability to improve their living conditions and status without violent interference or repression by the old elite. Furtado therefore believes that in the open industrial sector of society, gradualism is the appropriate method of change; however, in the rigid agrarian sector, social objectives will tend to be achieved "by cataclysmic disruption."

Taken together, the studies of Bolivia and Brazil indicate that while revolution may be needed before change can take place in a rigid society, radical change may prevent revolution in an unevenly developed society.

Because underdeveloped countries are predominantly agricultural, the key change in an underdeveloped country is land reform. In "Land Reform and the Alliance for Progress," Edmundo Flores states that "the need for policies that will redistribute land and wealth in order to start economic development is generally accepted among economists. . . . Land reform in fact amounts to the adoption of a new pattern of income distribution: a capital levy on a few landlords that is distributed among many peasants and the state. This initial income shift greatly facilitates the increase of the domestic rate of capital formation, as proven spectacularly in the case of Mexico . . ." An examination of land reform and the economic growth of Mexico is therefore presented in order to illustrate the relationship between land reform and economic development.

Not all observers who think that revolution is a likely concomitant of economic development believe that the United States ought to encourage private investment in countries undergoing revolutions or directly aid revolutionary governments. Professor Bronfenbrenner argues that "It is questionable whether the lagging countries can be expected permanently to eschew the device of confiscating capital under their control unless capital is made available to them from abroad in large amounts at attractive terms; it is likewise questionable whether such largesse is in the economic interest of the lending countries." If confiscation is an immediate threat, provision of aid or investment gives underdeveloped countries "hostages," for the underdeveloped countries are enabled to demand more aid as a bribe to prevent confiscation of existing investments. By continually extracting aid by threatening expropriation, underdeveloped countries can force the West to finance the economic development of the "borrowing" countries "until the borrowing country has achieved development at a rate satisfactory to its leaders." Professor Bronfenbrenner therefore suggests that the West cut its losses and withdraw from the underdeveloped countries, except those in which confiscation is not likely to occur in the near future.

The articles discussed so far suggest that revolution both must and inevitably will take place in many countries before economic development can begin. In strong disagreement, a number of authors assert that gradual changes in both the political and the economic structure of a country should take the place of revolution: carefully contrived reforms and economic planning are declared to be the alternative to violence. Professor Hirschman discusses the ways in which evolutionary changes can be contrived; he believes that reforms should not be presented as an integrated "package-deal," lest the opponents of each element of the reform combine to defeat the reform package. Instead, reforms should be presented piece-meal, in sequence, so that each reform can be passed by a different constellation of pro-reform forces. Revolutionaries, by insisting on total change at once, are not able to obtain any of the changes involved. Nonetheless, the presence of revolutionaries is necessary to frighten conservatives into an alliance with reformers; the resulting coalition agrees to institute reforms gradually, so that more extreme change can be avoided. In Hirschman's view, in order to obtain social and economic change necessary for economic development, revolutionaries are necessary, but revolution is not.

Economic development can be facilitated not only by evolutionary political change, but also by a more rational and efficient use of resources within existing economic and political structures. In "Planning and the Underdeveloped Countries," Gunnar Myrdal argues that "as economic development cannot be expected to come by itself, planning becomes a pre-condition for development, not, as in the Western countries, a later consequence of development and all the other changes which accompanied it." In addition to increasing the rate of growth, planning can be used to direct economic growth and benefits to the least stable sectors of society, and thus to reduce the threat of revolution.

The final two selections present country studies which evaluate the relative efficacy of revolution and evolution as methods of economic growth. Attempts to relate ideology and revolution to economic development are presented in these two essays. Malenbaum and Stolper compare the economic results of Communist revolutions in

East Germany and China to the economic results of non-totalitarian change in West Germany and India. The authors believe that Communist China and West Germany were the two more successful nations because "they geared their development programs to the existing structure of their economies." Flexibility of approach, rather than ideology, was the key to success.

In the final selection, "Economic Development Policies and Argentine Economic Growth," Randall suggests that frequent economic policy shifts "yielded neither sustained rapid economic growth nor preferred treatment by foreign lenders." The failure to obtain desired growth rates has been the result of each socio-economic group's attempt to maintain its relative share of power and income. Since economic development brings with it changes in the shares of power and income going to differing social groups, attempts to preserve the *status quo* inhibit economic growth. As a result, Argentine society must be transformed before economic growth can take place.

PART ONE

THE ECONOMIC AND POLITICAL BACKGROUND

INTRODUCTION

The general economic case for revolution as a precondition of economic development is presented in "Social and Economic Revolution for the Development of Backward Countries" by J. E. P. Belshaw. He argues that among the factors repressing growth within the present structure of many underdeveloped countries are the small scale of markets, the inadequate supply and quality of entrepreneurs, and social and political conditions that inhibit market-oriented behaviour. Further, Western technology may not be suited to local conditions, while the West itself may appear more attractive to investors than their own country. As a result, economic development cannot be left to the free play of the market or to the guidance of the entrepreneur. Even if the economic growth that takes place under private enterprise were of the same kind that takes place under government direction, its pace would be too slow.

It follows that in order to speed up economic development, the government must take over leadership functions from the entrepreneur. It becomes important to develop a nationalist ideology that validates state actions taken in order to increase the rate of economic growth. This point is discussed in the second selection, "Nationalism and Economic Development," by Yusif Sayigh.

J. E. P. Belshaw is Professor of Economics at the University of New Zealand. Yusif Sayigh is the author of *The Economic Impact of the Arab Refugee Problem on Lebanon, Syria, and Jordan,* and of *Entrepreneurs of Lebanon—The Business Leader in a Developing Economy.*

1

J. E. P. BELSHAW

Social and Economic Revolution
for the Development of
Backward Countries*

THE backward countries are now engaged in an attempt to achieve quickly and by direction what Western countries achieved in two hundred years and more through the initiative of countless individuals under free enterprise. Success in this attempt will depend upon drastic changes in the domestic balance of power, upon an internal revolution affecting every detail of the political and social structure, and upon a change in population trends. When the economic development of backward countries depends upon internal changes of this nature and magnitude, it is doubtful if the West can play more than a minor role in bringing economic progress about. . . . It is one problem to understand the past growth of a Western economy; it is another to bring about growth in a backward economy that has not acquired a similar social climate and institutions. "No past experience however rich and no historical research however thorough can save the living generation the creative task of finding their own answers and shaping their own future.". . .

Whatever the value of [econometric] models in a Western environment there is no disputing their limited usefulness in the environment of a backward country. Indeed, there is a growing conviction there that the essential conditions and postulates of Western economic theory, both static and dynamic, born in industrial Europe and America, are inapplicable in backward countries. The problem there is not to provide models of change but to bring growth about. Social climate and institutions cannot be taken for granted; a change in them is a necessary condition of economic change itself; experience gained in Western capitalism may be of limited usefulness in pre-capitalistic societies. Moreover, where the problem is to achieve development on a

* *Economic Record*, vol. XXXII #63 (November 1956). Reprinted by permission of The Economic Society of Australia and New Zealand.

broad front in a hitherto stagnant economy, the normal procedure in Western countries of examining problems piecemeal is of limited usefulness. By contrast with the reception of much of modern economics, classical economics in an earlier day had an appeal to the awakening intelligentsia of the East. Recently an economic historian has said that "looked at from the present day, the *Wealth of Nations,* in one of its aspects, is a dynamic analysis and programme of policy for an underdeveloped country." There is, indeed, beginning with Adam Smith, a broad, though broken, tradition that, while not providing a programme of development for backward countries, may provide a theoretical framework that may help us to put together more easily the various pieces of the puzzle and give us a sense of direction.

Smith regarded production as the struggle of man against nature and progress a measure of his success in this struggle. Economic progress depended upon increased division of labour, brought about by an extension of the market and the accumulation of capital. Malthus (*Principles of Political Economy,* Book 2) was concerned to explain why the "powers of production" could not result in the growth of wealth unless they were united with the "means of distribution" through an extension of trade, an adaptation of goods to wants that coaxed man out of his indolence, a distribution of income that avoided a concentration of wealth, the rise of a middle class, and the growth of services. . . .

Growth is retarded by the slow adaptation of men to change, by the need for a new geographical distribution of population, and by the slow formation of capital. . . . Nurkse . . . argues [that] in a poor country [there is] a circular constellation of forces tending to act and react upon one another in such a way as to keep a poor country in a state of poverty. Capital formation and investment is low, not because there is no need — the need is obvious — but because the inducement to invest is low. It is low because poverty limits the size of the market. The size of the market is small because there is no investment and capital formation and the changes that go with it. To put it tritely "a country is poor because it is poor." The social desirability of investment is high but private investment depends upon profit expectations. These are low because new investment is not supported by others and by the consequent expansion of the market characteristic of the West in the past. Hence there are "strong arguments for believing that the rate of development may be speeded up if the market as the governing mechanism of economic progress is eliminated and if investments are affected according to a coordinated plan. . . ."

It is true that in the latter half of the nineteenth century private investors from Britain were investing annually large sums overseas and that by 1913 this amounted annually to 7 per cent of the British national income. But this was an episode that cannot be repeated. The flow was to areas of recent settlement with vast resources; it was accompanied by a migration of 60 m. people already equipped with advanced industrial skills and carrying with them a cultural environment favourable to enterprise; the greater portion of it was invested in public utility and government securities particularly for the construction of railways.

It is improbable that private capital will be forthcoming in similar proportions to meet the very different needs of the twentieth century. The investment of private capital in backward countries could, indeed, have considerable advantages. It has been described as a "package-deal" contributing foreign exchange, know-how, risk-bearing and entrepreneurship, all scarce elements in backward countries. Though some backward countries appreciate it is to their advantage to encourage private investment by taking such steps to improve the security of such investments, the political and social circumstances are discouraging. Private investors prefer to invest their funds in advanced countries where the security is better and the returns are likely to be higher. What private foreign investment there is in backward countries continues to follow the traditional pattern of investment in extractive industries for export. While private investments of this type do make a contribution to development it is not great: they do little to penetrate the economy with new skills; they seldom stimulate cumulative rounds of investments; they seldom raise local incomes significantly. The backward countries suspect that the gains from such investments have gone mainly to the West. The preference for investment in extractive industries for export is clear from Nurkse's analysis. Profitable markets exist overseas but the internal market in terms of real incomes is small and cannot be greatly expanded without a co-ordinated programme of investment. If private investors are unable and unwilling to provide more than a small fraction of the funds required, it is possible that foreign governments and international institutions might provide them. In 1950, for example, the United States provided a $4½ billion in grants and loans to foreign governments. That was a substantial amount but it was less than one-third of the amount suggested by the United Nations experts. It is unlikely that other Western countries would be both able and willing to provide the additional amount. The bulk of the funds would thus have to come from the United States. Loans or grants of the size suggested on an annual basis for a lengthy period of time appear to be most improbable. Furthermore, of the amounts provided in loans and grants in the year taken, 80 per cent went to Europe to help in the reconstruction of a society already industrialized and equipped with advanced skills. The transfer of such amounts to backward countries before the social and cultural environment was prepared might involve a colossal waste of resources. Even so, the amount suggested by the United Nations experts represents an amount that is only a fraction of the annual net investment per head in advanced countries. This analysis is not intended to imply either that foreign capital cannot play a part in the development programmes of backward countries or that we are rendering the maximum amount of help within our power but rather to suggest that foreign financial aid can play only a subsidiary part and that the greater part must be played by the backward countries themselves. If this is so, then three problems arise concerned with the sources of capital within backward countries, the economies that can be achieved in capital use, and the mechanism by which the processes of growth can be started.

The low level of workers' incomes in backward countries provides little excess for savings above the barest minimum of subsistence while the demonstration effects of higher standards of living and the untouchability of goods beyond their means encourages a revolutionary feeling of frustration rather than any desire to save. The small middle-class that exists in most backward countries tends to ape the spending habits of their social betters. There is in most backward countries a small class of very wealthy people but their habits are usually characterized by high spending, conspicuous consumption, investment in land, real estate or in non-productive capital formation, combined with disdain for frugal habits of enterprise. Something may be and is being achieved in some countries to mobilize savings that can be made available from these sources by propaganda, the establishment of suitable savings institutions, heavy taxation, and sumptuary or other laws restricting spending. The largest class in any backward country is the peasantry, and there may be the temptation to obtain by duress, taxation or other means as heavy a proportion of their output as possible to feed the growing class of workers in the towns and to assist in capital formation, but Soviet experience has suggested what the dangers may be in unsympathetic attitudes towards the peasantry. . . . An increase in the productivity of agriculture is fundamental in any programme of development, though this was not sufficiently realized in the earlier programmes for development. Faced with small capital and taxable resources and impatient with a slow rate of progress, the governments of backward countries may be tempted to create "forced" savings by the creation of new money. This might give quick results in expanding production if idle capital capacity exists, but this is rarely the case in backward countries. Capital equipment has to be created or otherwise obtained before a flow of goods to the market is achieved. In the meantime inflationary effects are likely to be seen in price rises, an increase in imports, and the depletion of reserves of foreign currency, unless the policy is also associated with price and import control, rationing and additional taxation. The scarcity of capital indicates the need for economy in its use. . . .

One of the difficulties in industrialization in backward countries is that existing techniques have been mainly formed in the West as the result of a long series of innovations reflecting both a high level of skill and a great consumption of capital. In backward countries inferior rather than advanced techniques are often the more suitable; borrowing of techniques from another backward economy is frequently more profitable than attempting to use Western methods; engineering research, unhampered by Western traditions, needs to be directed to the development of techniques suitable for the very different circumstances of primitive societies. The principle that economies in the use of capital are necessary is similar to but narrower in scope than the principle that the allocation of capital between investments should be on the basis of their marginal productivity. Like so many propositions in economics, the principle is easier to state than to use as the basis of policy. If we were concerned with additions to the world's wealth and not with reductions in inequalities between nations investment in the already wealthy countries would be the policy usually indicated. Similarly when foreign capital seeks investment in export industries and shuns investments for the internal market it is because marginal productivity or profits is higher in the former. A different result follows when the criterion becomes social rather than private marginal productivity. Firstly, as Nurkse pointed out, the social profitability of an investment often exceeds its private profitability since it may assist in the formation of an environment more suitable in general, implying that in the early stages of development investment cannot be left to be guided by private profits alone. Secondly, investment returns, both private and social, depend upon the existence of a physical capital framework, notably transport, communication, power production, and the like. The direct return on these investments may be less than the annual charges yet their contribution to development is very great. Private marginal productivity is not a suitable criterion. The fact that such investments are highly capital intensive suggests also that economy in capital use does not always mean small capital use. Thirdly, investment in human beings is likely to be the most socially profitable of all investments though the criterion of private marginal productivity hardly applies at all. This focuses attention upon one of the many dilemmas in development, the conflict between heavy short-period cost and large but delayed returns. It may sometimes be resolved not by the use of the usual Western techniques but by the techniques devised, for example, for mass education in an illiterate society. Unless the concept of social marginal productivity is extended, there is one major exception to it as a matter of necessity. Development will involve the import of capital equipment from the West. Increases in incomes generated by expansion will also result in an increased demand for imported consumption goods. Development programmes are therefore likely to involve both investment in export producing or import replacing industries and a close supervision of the earnings of foreign currency. It is especially here that foreign loans or grants have an important part to play. . . .

Lewis sees as the central problem in development the process by which a low rate of saving is converted into a high rate and directed into productive capital formation. The answer lies in the use of the capitalist surplus acquired from rents and profits. Rents are owned by a small wealthy class living luxuriously, opposed to the interests of the middle class, and fearful of the social consequences of changes. Profits by their very origin are more likely to be used productively in capital formation and in financing innovation. The problem of increasing the rate of capital formation then, suggests Lewis, becomes the problem of increasing the size of the capitalistic sector in the economy. An increase in the size of this sector depends upon an improvement in the quality and quantity of the entrepreneurial factor, but favourable changes in the social environment and the extension of the market necessary to bring this about can be achieved slowly only. In the meantime entrepreneurship will remain scarce and defective in quality. It is a strange comment upon American aid to backward countries born in an atmosphere of free enterprise that these difficulties have sometimes turned American economic officials overseas into social revolutionaries. The accumulation of a capitalist surplus may then become the responsibility of the state under a system of state capitalism. It is here that we are likely to be disappointed if our aid to backward countries is based on the belief that it will lead to the growth of an economic system similar to our own. Rather our hope should be that state capitalism as well as increasing standards of living will favour and protect those human freedoms we believe to be valuable. In any case state capitalism or at the very least a greater measure of state activity than we are accustomed to is likely to be necessary before there is an environment favourable to the rapid growth of a private enterprise sector. Provided state capitalism or private capitalism both protect the freedoms we believe to be valuable then they become, from our point of view, no more than a means and the fact that free enterprise has given us our own high standards of living should not blind us to the fact that it may not be capable of achieving the same standards elsewhere. But, unfortunately, we cannot assume that all governments have the willingness or ability to take the necessary steps or give an effective lead. Baran, after an examination of the social environment and the distribution of political powers characteristic of many backward countries, wrote: "The crucial fact rendering the realization of a developmental programme illusory is the political and social structure of the governments in power. The alliance of property-owning classes controlling the destinies of most underdeveloped countries cannot be expected to design and to execute a set of measures running counter to each and all of their immediate vested interests. If, to appease the restive public, blueprints of progressive measures such as agrarian reform, equitable tax legislation, etc., are officially announced, their enforcement is wilfully sabotaged. The government, representing a political compromise between landed and business interests, cannot suppress the wasteful management of landed estates and the conspicuous consumption on the part of the aristocracy, cannot suppress monopolistic abuses, profiteering, capital flights, and extravagant living on the part of the businessmen. It cannot curtail or abandon its lavish appropriations for military and police establishments, providing attractive careers to the scions of wealthy families and a profitable outlet for armaments produced by their parents — quite apart from the fact that this establishment serves as the main protection against possible popular revolt. Set up to guard and to abet the existing property rights and privileges, it cannot become the architect of a policy calculated to destroy the privileges, it cannot become the architect of economic progress and to place the property and the incomes derived from it at the service of society as a whole." No doubt this is an exaggerated picture of the situation in many countries. Nevertheless it is true that economic progress may in some countries depend upon a social revolution difficult to spark and difficult to control. In such countries financial assistance from overseas by assisting those in power may sometimes hinder rather than assist progress.

YUSIF SAYIGH

Nationalism and
Economic Development*

CAN private entrepreneurs not *initiate* development without all this business of shocks, thrusts, and breakthroughs? My answer is "No." Underdevelopment is a complex phenomenon; its roots and its manifestations extend beyond the area of economics. So of necessity do the remedies for it and the agencies that prescribe and administer the *first* remedies. The phenomenon as it burdens the world today is unlike that which burdened the developed countries of the West in their pre-industrial age. Troubled by its many political and social insecurities, economic shortages, and organizational rigidities, the underdeveloped environment of today blocks private entrepreneurs from performing the economic and technological functions that devolved upon their counterparts in the West in the heyday of private enterprise and free competition.

Furthermore, because of the pressures of national aspirations and of the urgency of social and economic reform, few backward societies can wait while private enterprise builds up momentum slowly, firm by firm and product by product, ultimately to carry the economy to a reasonably high level of performance. Only very slow progress can be registered if the broad framework for enterprise changes slowly; and it can change but slowly at the hands of ruling groups that are not social-minded and that do not take upon themselves the leadership of social and economic forces striving for reform. But slow change is a poor response to the sense of crisis that hammers impatiently at the door of backward systems today. Little trust can therefore be placed in private enterprise to be the *prime mover* in the process of development.

Where success in initiating this process has been achieved in the past few decades, the pressure for action, and later the action, have almost invariably come from an articulate and activist minority in

---

* From "Development: The Visible or the Invisible Hand?," *World Politics*, vol. XIII #4 (July 1961). Reprinted by permission of *World Politics*.

society.[1] This minority has proved to be both sensitive to the humiliation of poverty and backwardness, and restless in the determination to express its protest in concrete acts through the instrumentality of the state. Whether stirred more by deep resentment and bitterness or by positive social-mindedness, whether given to dictatorial tendencies or imbued with liberal ideas, this group discovers, none too soon, that concrete acts can be taken only by those who assure themselves of political authority. Anyone who refuses to admit this inevitable fact will find himself well outside the inner circle of decision-makers.

The members of the leadership who ultimately converge on the center of political power come from different backgrounds. There are intellectuals and professional men; civil servants, party leaders, and idealistic politicians; revolutionaries and young army officers. Increasingly it is army officers who swiftly, and conveniently, seize power and make use of the ideas, skills, and services of the other members of the leadership group who are acceptable to the military. But what is more significant than the identity of the ruling group is the fact that it is almost invariably motivated in its drive for economic development by a political and social ideology of power and welfare, rather than by private profit. In one sentence, the ideology is one of national resurgence, involving power for the state and dignity and well-being for the citizen.

The supremacy of nationalist ideology is the most common feature of these countries seeking and designing development. A pattern can be observed in the experience of the Kemalist revolution in Turkey, as in the orderly take-over by the Congress Party in India, in Nuri es-Said's patriarchal domination of Iraq as in Nasser's social revolution in Egypt, in Mexico as in Cuba, in Syria as in the Sudan or in Pakistan — regardless of the differences in emphasis underlying the philosophy of action, in the directions in which the initial thrust may have turned, or in the varying degree of success as between one country and another.

Nationalism in most underdeveloped regions of the world is truly explosive. Pressing in pre-industrial societies where the industrial revolution has been delayed, it can, and not infrequently does, explode in political revolutions.[2] But this is only half the truth.

---

[1] Foreign national minorities, to whom some writers attribute an important role in technological change and development, are indeed invaluable. But, as private entrepreneurs, they emerge only later, after the initial thrust has been made.

[2] Writing about the USSR, Gerschenkron has said that "The delayed industrial revolution was responsible for a political revolution." . . . Equally true is

Without the discontent and the desire for change that set off revolution, these societies remain far from the threshold of the industrial revolution. Neither the appropriate ideology and dynamism, nor the leadership of social and economic development have emerged or operated in any underdeveloped country in the past few decades without a revolution. Revolution — it remains to be said — need not be one of iron and blood; but even if it is one of ideas, it has to involve a radical shift in the pattern of power to enable the leadership groups to come to the center of authority.[3]

This trend is clearly a cardinal fact in Middle East society. The state, now the master of economic destiny, is in fact the vehicle of the ideas and ambitions and hopes of leaders. Even if initially the state seems to be the embodiment, not the vehicle, of these ideas and ambitions and hopes, it still remains an avowed vehicle, the express objective being the multi-sided liberation of the individual in society. But now, and for some time to come, the observer will have to keep his eyes focused on the center of political power, the ideology underlying political and social action, and the men wielding the power and professing the ideology, for an understanding of the drive for and the directions and quality of economic development.

The role of the leadership at this initial stage is multiple. It is first to articulate social discontent — even, or perhaps especially, of the mute mass, whose discontent is principally silent and sullen — and simultaneously to promise redress. Next, the role is to produce the dogma, the faith, or merely the avenues of action imperative for social and economic reform. Almost invariably this reform presupposes political reform. Where caution is the better part of valor, political reform is not demanded publicly. But when zero hour strikes and power is taken by bullet or by poll, the political component of reform is expounded. With the take-over of power the men in leadership move to the position of responsibility, of decision-making. All their previous attitudes, philosophy, expressions, and schemes are a

the fact [Sic! — Ed.] that it was the political revolution that made possible the full fruition of the industrial revolution in the USSR.

[3] Only rarely do the old, established leaderships accept some of the new ideas and incorporate them in their philosophy of action. The ruling group in Iraq tried this in the early 1950's; the ruling group in Iran in the mid-1950's; the ruling group in Turkey all through the 1950's. In these and other cases, some political and social ideas of great significance to the articulate minorities were left out. Hence the revolutions of Iraq and Turkey which Iran has so far been spared. Christ's saying about the futility of putting new wine in old bottles is still as good as when He uttered it.

mere prelude to the next part of their role. Even if they keep much of the ideas and the philosophy, the phase upon which they enter is predominantly one of activism. While in the earlier, preparatory phase they may have been judged mainly by what they believed and said, in the activist phase they will be judged mainly by what they do or fail to do.

Their role in this second phase requires them to establish nationalist resurgence as their mission and the state as the only possible agent of this mission. To this end, the state must be established as the source of inspiration and of authority for action. Apart from the consolidation of law and order, this means that the state has to have a "presence" — its image must be built up as a source of power, knowledge, wisdom, resourcefulness. The state knows best and is surest to succeed: this becomes the philosophy of economic action and the bridge of communication between the ruler and the ruled. It remains to be said that this "line" is not difficult to establish in societies where the economic role of the state has always been extensive and its authority generally accepted.[4]

Only the cynic would disparage this "line." The need of the hour largely justifies this exaggeration of roles. Furthermore, since the leadership can hardly stop at this point but has to move farther in its efforts, the assumption of extensive powers by the state seems to be well justified. Intent on development, the leadership proceeds to equip society with the setting for the directly producing sectors of the economy (that is, the sectors which conventionally belong in the area of private enterprise in Western industrial countries, for the evolution of which economic and social overhead capital is created). Education and technical training are emphasized, roads are built, business legislation is enacted, land reform is undertaken, resources are developed, capital is accumulated. And all this is usually attempted within the framework of a broad plan of development covering the whole territory of the country.

At this stage the leadership does not wait long for private entrepreneurs to enter industry, transport, communications, mining, or banking, but itself embarks on projects in these and other fields, without inhibition. Nevertheless, the setting will have been prepared by then for the more daring, and later for the more cautious, among

---

[4] In societies where a traditional attitude of "God will provide" predominates, a shift to the attitude of "The state will provide" cannot be very difficult to make.

businessmen to enter the non-traditional fields of economic activity.[5] Normally, businessmen begin gradually to take over from here on, by increasingly entering the directly productive sectors and industries. With a little help or, better still, with the confidence that security is the order of the day, that their efforts will receive decent reward, and that the reward will remain largely theirs, businessmen can be instrumental in developing further the directly productive sectors and industries. Within broad limits of social policy, they are worthy of every encouragement, both because of the value of their contribution to growth, and because their activity will relieve the government of part of the burden of its role as a supplier of business enterprise.

Frequently, unsure that some or all of their expectations will materialize, businessmen balk. Gladly or reluctantly, depending on the economic philosophy of the leadership and its own opinions and expectations of business, the state agency may step in. On occasion, and the occasions grow by the day, the state in its overeagerness for results steps in even before private enterprise has had a chance to decide either way, or even after it has moved in with energy. But the case of private enterprise vs. state enterprise, with its attendant question of timing, is only one of the issues or debates that arise from the breakthrough by the leadership and the role of the state it necessitates.

[5] Up to this point, business risks are likely to be oppressive and inhibiting, except for the most daring of entrepreneurs. Moreover, "Where risks are great, only the biggest bureaucracy can carry on, and not uncommonly this has been the state. As risks lessen, the private firm with state support is enabled to invest with some hope of commensurate return. It is only in unique environments that state action may retreat well into the background, with some allowance for lag in the process." . . .

PART TWO

THE CASE FOR REVOLUTION

INTRODUCTION

Many observers believe that revolution is not only a precondition for economic development, but also that nationalist revolutions in underdeveloped countries are inevitable. The following four selections present the case for revolution in differing historical contexts. For example, when the social structure of a country is rigid, and decisions are largely made by an oligarchy devoted to preserving an appalling *status quo* which prevents economic development, then revolution is likely to occur as a necessity before any development can take place. Carter Goodrich evaluates the argument for revolution in an oligarchic society in "Revolution and Economic Development."

Many countries, however, cannot be described either as oligarchies with no social mobility or as democracies with considerable opportunity to move up the social ladder. Developing nations often contain some oligarchic elements and exhibit some social mobility; further, the way in which a developing nation is organized may differ considerably among its component regions. It is possible that the most backward part of a nation will be transformed by revolution, while the more developed regions may grow by more peaceful methods. Celso Furtado describes the wide range of factors that must be taken into account in selecting among peaceful and violent techniques of development, and follows this discussion by specific examples taken from Brazil.

A major component of a nationalist revolution is the redistribution of property rights. In an agrarian society, land ownership is often the dominant form of ownership of wealth-producing assets, so that redistribution of property rights takes the form of agrarian reform.

Edmundo Flores presents the need for land reform as a key element in economic development, with particular reference to Latin American nations and the Alliance for Progress.

How are property rights redistributed? By gift or sale—perhaps. But in poor countries, Martin Bronfenbrenner believes that redistribution of property is apt to take place by confiscation—first of foreigners' property, then of nationals' property. Many of the points made in his analysis of the appeal of confiscation in economic development have been borne out by events subsequent to the publication of his article in 1955. The author's conclusion — that since confiscation often appears to be an inevitable part of the process of economic development, United States government policy should be economic neo-isolationism or withdrawal from a large number of areas — is still the subject of considerable debate.

Professor Carter Goodrich was actively engaged in the United Nations technical assistance program for Bolivia from 1949 to 1953. During 1952–1953 he was in charge of the program as the special representative of the Secretary General, when the Bolivian Revolution began. This experience provides the background for his article "Revolution and Economic Development."

Celso Furtado has served as head of the Northeast Development Agency (SUDENE) and Minister of Planning in the Brazilian Cabinet. His study of Brazil's economic development, *The Economic Growth of Brazil,* was published in the United States in 1963.

Professor Edmundo Flores teaches agricultural economics at the School of Economics, the National Autonomous University of Mexico. He served with the United Nations technical assistance program in Bolivia. Professor Martin Bronfenbrenner teaches at the Carnegie Institute of Technology.

CARTER GOODRICH

Revolution and
Economic Development[*]

The Bolivian Revolution of 1952 opened with a burst of rifle and machine-gun fire at daybreak on the Wednesday of Easter week. The firing ceased on the afternoon of Good Friday and a new government was in possession of the capital city of La Paz.

It is this revolution and its consequences that I wish to analyze, since they have a profound bearing on the nature and the prospects of economic development in the country. For this was a real revolution, different both in origins and in program from the eighty or so earlier overturns that had taken place since Bolivia achieved independence from Spain a century and a quarter before. Most of these revolutions, like many others elsewhere in Latin America, had involved little more than a changing of the palace guard. In the typical case, one leader and his friends won over part of the army and displaced another similar group, sometimes by bitter fighting, sometimes by a bloodless coup in which a strategically placed battalion or regiment took possession of the Presidential Palace. When it was over, the defeated leaders usually fled or were sent into exile, with the result that a large proportion of the men of education and ability were at any given time outside their own country. In most of these overturns, each of the contending groups was drawn from the same limited number of leading families or from the cadre of ambitious army officers. Ordinarily neither group possessed great popular backing, and the change from one to the other brought no substantial alteration of national policies.

At its outset, the Easter week uprising of 1952 followed in part this characteristic pattern. It was touched off by the defection from the existing government of its Minister of the Interior, himself a

[*] From "The Economic Transformation of Bolivia," New York State School of Industrial and Labor Relations, *Bulletin* 34 (October, 1955). Reprinted by permission of the author and of the New York State School of Industrial and Labor Relations.

general, who controlled the military police. But when the revolt appeared to be losing and when detachments of the regular army loyal to the old regime appeared to be gaining the upper hand, the General eliminated himself by taking asylum in the Chilean Embassy, a privilege which forms part of the standard institutional pattern of the Latin American revolution. His *caribinieros* continued fighting. But from the beginning most of the men — and women — who carried arms in the rebellion were civilians — miners, trade unionists, and other wage earners of the city, small shopkeepers and members of the middle class, all of them members of or sympathizers with an organized political party. When the fighting ended, it was this party, and not the defecting general, who organized the new government.

The party was the Nationalist Revolutionary Movement, *Movimiento Nacionalista Revolucionario,* known by its initials as the M.N.R. It had formed a part of an earlier government, that of President Villaroel, which had itself been ousted by revolution in 1946. Five years later, although its principal leaders were in exile — again in conformity with the traditional pattern — the M.N.R. nevertheless won the largest number of votes in the elections of May 1951. It came out far ahead of its closest rival but fell just short of the clear majority required for automatic election. Before the Congress could act, the then President abdicated and turned over his power to a Military Junta of generals and colonels, which was organized for the express purpose of keeping the *Movimiento* out of office. It was this Junta which fell in April 1952; and it was the M.N.R.'s candidates of 1951, Dr. Víctor Paz Estenssoro and Dr. Hernán Siles Zuazo, who became President and Vice-President under the new regime. President Paz Estenssoro, a former Professor of Economics who had been Minister of Finance under Villaroel, had directed the revolutionary movement from exile in Buenos Aires and Montevideo. Dr. Siles had led the revolt inside the country with the strong support of the miners' leader, Señor Juan Lechín.

By the double test of votes and arms, the Nationalist Revolutionary Movement had demonstrated a considerable basis of public support. The first test affected only the small upper- and middle-class group to which the franchise was limited under the requirement of literacy. The second showed the adherence of the miners and other popular groups, though not yet of the still unpolitical Indians of the land. The party boasted of its support by what it called *las clases mayoritarias,* the majority classes; and its first cabinet included Señor Lechín of the miners and Señor Germán Butrón of the textile workers' union. One of the first institutions organized after the revolution was the Workers' Central, the *Central Obrera Boliviana*, which exerted considerable influence over the government and became a powerful pressure group for higher wages, family allowances, and increased social insurance.

The program announced by the party was definite and drastic. It contained two principal planks. The first was the nationalization of the mines of the three great tin companies. The second was a land reform that would break up the large estates and transfer the land to the possession of the Indians.

Considering the nature of the Bolivian economy and the structure of Bolivian society, as I have attempted to outline them, it would be hard to imagine more far-reaching proposals. No two measures could have involved greater economic and political hazards. Tin was the country's one great source of dollar income, and four fifths of the tin was mined by the Patiño, Hochschild, and Aramayo companies, largely under the direction of foreign managers and technicians. Since their ownership also had by this time become almost entirely foreign, expropriation might imperil Bolivia's position in the capitalistic world. It would risk a loss of markets, and it could hardly fail to discourage foreign investments on which future development would depend.

From the point of view of the internal life of the country, the land reform appeared to present even greater dangers. It ran directly counter to the interests of the one powerful class within the country, great landowners, who had provided most of the nation's political and intellectual leadership and even the greater part of such attempts as had been made for the development of local business enterprise. Land reform would risk their complete alienation. At the same time, it would hazard the future of the nation's food supply very largely on the unknown and uncertain capacities and disposition of the Indian population.

Whatever the risks, the new government went forward with its announced program. On October 31, 1952, a decree was promulgated nationalizing the mining interests of the Patiño, Hochschild, and Aramayo companies. The decree accepted the principle of compensation and provided that a portion of the proceeds of the mines should be set aside for this purpose. But it also included provisions for examining various counterclaims against the companies, ranging from charges of avoidance of back taxes to claims of compensation for the families of miners killed in the course of industrial disputes. There was sufficient ambiguity in the language of the decree and in the declarations of some of the leaders to raise doubts as to whether compensation would in fact be given.

For us as observers or as historians, it is important to attempt to understand why so drastic a step was undertaken. The motives were no doubt complex. Among them doctrinaire socialism, socialism of the books, could hardly have played an important part. It was scarcely a logical application of socialist theory to nationalize three companies within an industry and to leave the various middle-sized concerns and the host of small mines — the *chicos* — in private hands. At the same time, indeed, the government was proclaiming its desire to encourage the introduction of private capital to assist in the development of the country, and it gave at least one concrete demonstration of this intention by offering private concessionaires the opportunity to enter the petroleum industry which itself had been nationalized by another government sixteen years before.

One part of the basis for nationalization lay in the bitter class hatred that had grown up in the labor conflicts in the mining camps and had been intensified by the violence on both sides. This feeling was dramatized by the promulgation of the decree, before a great gathering of miners, in a field near Catavi chosen because it had been the site of what the mine workers had regarded as a "massacre" of some of their fellows. Moreover, since the local management of the mines, though not the ultimate control of the companies, was so often in the hands of citizens of the United States, the miners' feeling was in part anti-gringo, anti-Yankee.

The preamble to the decree referred, as you would expect, to great profits sent abroad and derived from the irreplaceable natural resources of Bolivia. It spoke with particular bitterness of the fact that the companies had not chosen to reinvest their earnings in the development of other parts of the Bolivian economy. Public statements of the leaders declared that nationalization would give to the Bolivian people the economic benefits that had in the past gone to foreigners and expatriates. Yet some of those most active in framing the measure and pressing for its adoption were by no means certain that the government would succeed in drawing as much revenue from its own operation of the mines as it had obtained in taxation from the proceeds of their operation in private hands. For them, the compelling motive for insistence on nationalization was not economic but in the broadest sense political. As the one part of the Bolivian economy based on the exploitation of rich resources by modern methods and advanced technology, the three great companies had come to represent a concentration of economic power and financial resources far greater than those of the Bolivian government or of any other institution within the country. The preamble of the decree charged them with using this power to control elections and to make and un-make governments. Whatever the truth or falsehood of these allega-tions, however well or badly the power was in fact exercised, its very existence had come to seem intolerable to the Bolivian nationalist. To him it represented an *imperium in imperio* which had to be abol-ished if the nation was to be free to manage its own affairs.[1]

In my judgment, then — and perhaps you will find it the more credible if you compare the Bolivian action with similar movements in other parts of the world — the basis for nationalization was much less Socialist or Communist, and certainly much less anti-Yankee, than it was the expression of a militant nationalism. This was, I be-lieve, the compelling motive.

From nationalization, the government went on in the following year to carry out its program of the land reform. In this case, the decree was promulgated on August 2, 1953. It declared that three types of agricultural holding were of benefit to the country and should be preserved — small proprietorship, medium proprietorship, and the larger "agricultural enterprise" representing substantial capital invest-ment and progressive methods of cultivation. The traditional *latifun-dias* were to be abolished. The land taken was to be paid for over a term of years, and it was to be purchased on long terms by those to whom it was assigned. These transfers would of course take time, but two changes took place immediately. Unpaid labor was abol-ished — the service of three or four days' labor per week which the Indians customarily rendered to the landlord in exchange for the use of small parcels of land; and these parcels themselves came into full possession of the Indian families.

Because of what seems to me the extraordinary character of the social transformation which this measure attempts, the following lec-ture will be devoted to the relation of the Indian to the land. To this will be deferred any further discussion of the provisions of the land reform. It is, however, essential to the present argument to examine the motives underlying the decision. Advocacy of land reform was first of all based on the argument that the Indian's ancient wrongs should be redressed and that he should be fully incorporated into the eco-nomic, social, and political life of the nation. No doubt also the leaders of the M.N.R. believed that such treatment of the Indian would bring into Bolivian politics a new source of political strength that would help them to maintain their hard-won power. Consistent

[1] The Bolivian government's case is presented in *El Libro Blanco de la Inde-pendencia Económica de Bolivia* (La Paz, 1952).

with both these motives was the further decision of the government to enfranchise the Indian masses by extending the right to vote to all citizens regardless of literacy. But advocates of the land reform also hoped that the abolition of the unprogressive *latifundia* and the new incentives offered to the Indian landworkers would lead to a more efficient agriculture and to an increase in the nation's food supply.

If these were the purposes of the movement and these the measures taken, what were the problems that arose, what were the results, and what has been their bearing on the economic development? All these are continuing questions, to which much of the answer remains uncertain, but a part of the analysis must be attempted.

Let us begin with the mines. The nationalized properties were put into the hands of a government corporation, the *Corporación Minera de Bolivia*. One of its first problems was to provide supplies for the company stores, the *pulperías*, in the mining camps on which the subsistence of the miners depended. For this the new body lacked both the working capital of the companies and their systems of purchase and supply. The problem was met and the miners were fed, but for a time food was noticeably short in the cities of La Paz and Cochabamba.

A greater problem, of course, was that of operating and technical management, in which almost all of the major responsibilities had been held by foreigners. The government made strenuous efforts to keep these men, offering them security and the continuation of their contracts. In this, despite the earlier hostility between miners and managers, the *Corporación* was seconded by the Miners' Union. But the managers and engineers, either because of distrust of the new conditions or because of the terms of their contracts with the companies, for the most part refused these offers. More than two hundred left the country — North Americans, British, Dutch, German, and others; and these included almost every man who had been manager or chief engineer at a major operation.

On the side of the mine workers, the first reaction to nationalization seems to have been one of enthusiastic cooperation with the new regime. It was dramatized by an outdoor sunrise mass held on the Sunday of the decree on top of the famous hill of Potosí, now mined from tin instead of silver. The miners present made offerings and swore a great oath, now that the mines were the property of the Bolivian people, that they would increase production and even give up what had become a common practice — stealing ore from the mines! But this first enthusiasm, as would have been expected, tended to wear off. Though the industry has benefited since nationalization by the reduction in the number and seriousness of labor disputes, there seems to have been no sustained improvement in discipline. Wage costs, at least in local currency terms, have been pushed up under the pressure of the miners' union. The union also insisted on the re-employment of a number of miners who had left the mines, some of whom had been discharged for their part in the industrial disputes of the previous regime. The *Corporación's* payroll rose from 26,000 at the outset to about 37,000 toward the end of last year. Production per man, already lower than in other countries of Latin America, decreased still further.

Total production of the industry, on the other hand, has been well maintained since nationalization. The output of tin from all the mines, including those of the *Corporación*, was slightly greater in 1953 than in 1952. In the nationalized sector of the industry, though not in the private, the level of output was again maintained in 1954. Nor has this been, as some experts feared it might be, obtained by a policy of short-run robbing of the higher-grade ores. The Bolivian engineers, previously held down to minor posts within the industry, appear to have risen rather remarkably to their new responsibilities, with the aid of the minority of foreigners who remained and a few more who have been recruited. There remains a shortage of skilled mining and managerial personnel, and of competent mine foremen, but the results of nationalization have not borne out the widely held expectation that the industry would suffer physical deterioration or collapse.

Nor has the industry found itself cut off from its markets in Great Britain and the United States. There was some agitation within the country for expropriation without compensation, particularly on the part of a small but articulate Communist or Trotskyite minority within the Workers' Central. On the occasion of one trade union demonstration held in front of the *Palacio,* the President had to remind an orator from this group that Bolivia was a backward country located in America, without smelters for refining its ore, and that it was nonsense to "talk of tunnels to far-off countries for the export of our minerals." The President and his Cabinet, including the miners' leader, Señor Lechín who was also head of the Workers' Central, fully realized that terms had to be made with the mining companies.

A preliminary agreement was reached with the Patiño interests in June 1953. Under its terms, which were later extended to the other two companies, a fraction of the gross proceeds of the mines was to be set aside for compensation. The percentage was to vary with the price of tin, and payments were to be suspended if the latter should fall below eighty cents. The total amount of compensation was left for further negotiation. Before this agreement was reached, the United States government, one of Bolivia's two principal customers, had made several spot purchases of tin for its Texas City smelter, and agreed to a longer-term contract. As early as January of that year, the private English firm of Williams-Harvey in which the Patiño company held a large interest, contracted to purchase more than 50 percent of the Bolivian tin output for three years. Within a few months of nationalization, a Patiño smelter thus became again the purchaser of the product of the ex-Patiño mines.

Under the new contracts, the tin was to be bought at current world prices, not at the figure of $1.21½ that had previously been paid by the Reconstruction Finance Corporation. These prices were declining rapidly and fell even below the eighty-cent cutoff point of the contract with the companies. Thus payment of compensation was suspended but was resumed after a partial restoration of prices. The amount paid through 1954 is reported as $5,765,370.[2] Meanwhile, the fall in prices, together with the increased local costs to which I have referred, resulted in a considerable deficit for the nationalized mines, at least in domestic currency. More serious still, the effect of the drop from $1.20 to $.80 was to cut off suddenly almost a third of the dollar income on which Bolivia depended for its essential imports.

As a result, the financial plight of the country became desperate. It would in any case have been serious enough, with the problems of readjustment created by the government's own radical measures and with the difficulties it had inherited from the previous regime. These included an active inflation which continued to run unchecked. A determined effort to meet these problems was made in the measures of economic stabilization and exchange reform which were adopted in May 1953. By that time Bolivia had five official rates of foreign exchange, while the black-market dollar had risen to a point more than three times the highest of these and more than twelve times the lowest figure. Food came in at the bottom rate and at prices so low that much of it was promptly smuggled out again. Unless these conditions were changed, there could be little incentive for domestic agriculture and no hope of checking inflation, balancing the budget, or operating the mines on a reasonable basis. But there was no way to change them without causing serious hardship. The plan adopted established a single exchange rate for all imports and exports, made

[2] National Foreign Trade Corporation, *Noticias* (New York, Feb. 15, 1955), p. 7.

great increases in the duties on luxury imports, and set up a legal free market for other transactions. All this sent the cost of living sharply upward. The price of bread rose 150 percent. All salaries and wages, high and low, were increased by a flat amount, calculated roughly to compensate the lowest-paid workers for the increased costs. Everyone else was to bear a greater or lesser share of the new austerity.

An understanding of these measures, and of the attempts of the Bolivian government to promote the diversification and development of the economy, requires reference to the part played by the international organizations and by the government of the United States. A United Nations mission of technical assistance, as has been indicated, began work in Bolivia in the early months of 1952. Its position after the revolution was at first somewhat uncertain. Its original agreement had been made with the Military Junta, the enemies of the M.N.R., and leaders of the new government had criticized its arrangements for placing foreign experts in responsible positions within the Bolivian public service on the ground that this represented undue interference in the nation's internal affairs. Yet the eagerness of the new government to obtain help in its developmental projects made possible an adjustment of the program, and the very gravity of the economic problems led to an increasingly serious use of the counsel of the members of the mission.[3] Of this, the stabilization program was a notable example. The difficult political decision could only be taken by the President and the Cabinet, but the economic and technical preparation of the measures was mainly the work of the United Nations consultants in the Central Bank and the Ministry of Finance. A special mission of the International Monetary Fund cooperated on the exchange problem, and the measures were facilitated by a credit of $2,500,000 provided under the rules of the Fund.

In fields closer to the immediate interest of the School of Industrial and Labor Relations, other members of the mission assisted in the reorganization of the Ministry of Labor and in bringing order to an exceedingly chaotic system of social insurance. An expert from the International Labor Organization made arrangements under which groups of foremen and workers from the mines and oil fields were given periods of training and experience in other countries. Mining engineers, and more recently a metallurgist and a mineral geologist, have advised on costs and methods of mining. They recommended further exploitation of the baser minerals of lead, zinc, and copper,

[3] Carter Goodrich, "Bolivia: Test of Technical Assistance," *Foreign Affairs* (April 1954), pp. 473–481.

for which market prospects appeared more favorable than for tin. They also investigated the undeveloped iron resources of Mutún, which have since attracted the attention of a United States company. On the advice of one of these experts, the *Corporación Minera* is introducing into the mines a system of bonuses for productivity. Another United Nations technician investigated the possibility that Bolivia might profitably smelt a part of its own ores instead of sending the concentrates to England or the United States. This had been regarded as uneconomic because of the lack of cheap fuel, but now appears likely to be practicable on the basis of new processes depending on the use of water power. Here the work of this adviser dovetailed with that of the hydraulic engineer who devised plans which would utilize, as soon as substantial investment becomes possible, what he and others before him have regarded as the almost fabulous water resources of the eastern slope of the Cordillera. Other experts advised on agricultural policy, on road development, and on the business methods of the petroleum industry. When the Bolivian Development Corporation received bids for the construction of a new sugar mill — the largest single contract to be let in many years — its president invited the United Nations to send down two experts to help judge the bids in order to ensure expertness and objectivity.

The last case is significant in an interpretation of the government's policy toward development. In the year of the lowest tin price and of drastic restrictions on imports that almost stripped middle-class commodities from the shelves of La Paz merchants, the government took enough out of its meager store of foreign exchange to meet the first installment on the contract for the sugar mill, to cover its part of the cost of completing the Cochabamba road, and to purchase drilling equipment for the oil fields.

Yet if these actions indicate the determination of the Bolivian government to promote diversified development, it is also essential to point out that current progress in this direction — and perhaps even the avoidance of complete economic collapse — have been dependent on substantial and timely assistance given by the United States government. Emergency aid in the amount of eleven or twelve million dollars, largely in the form of surplus food, was furnished during the fiscal year 1953–1954. In addition the United States program of bilateral technical assistance, already substantial, was increased by a special allocation of two million dollars, to be used mainly for agricultural equipment. For the current fiscal year, emergency aid, aside from technical assistance, will amount to sixteen or eighteen million dollars.

A letter from President Eisenhower to President Paz Estenssoro, announcing the first of these decisions, said that the action was being taken because of the emergency created by the sudden drop in the world price of tin but also because of the fact that the government of Bolivia was "already taking wise and courageous measures looking toward the diversification and stabilization of the Bolivian economy." Programs for the application of this aid have been decided upon after the fullest possible consultation between United States officials and the Bolivian government. The plans for the present year, I am informed, were based on a memorandum of some hundred and thirty pages in which the government analyzed the prospects and shortcomings of the Bolivian economy, presented a realistic foreign exchange budget, and put forward its specific plans for economic development.

Priority has been given to aid in those fields in which there was hope of returns that would be quickly reflected in the balance of payments, particularly by reducing the need for imports. This meant mainly agriculture and petroleum. It is worth noting that United States assistance has been concentrated on the lines suggested more than ten years ago in the Bohan Report, which found the solution for the problems of Bolivian diversification in the building of an all-weather highway to open up the fertile plains of the Oriente. Now the Cochabamba-Santa Cruz road — for which the government had received loans of $44,000,000 from the Export-Import Bank — has finally been completed. Both the economic aid and the increased technical assistance on the part of the United States have been concentrated on the development of this new frontier of the world's farming. A rental pool of clearing, cultivating, and harvesting machinery has been established in the area by the Agricultural *Servicio* and a system set up for giving supervised agricultural credit. Large acreages of new land are being broken in. It is as yet too early to assess the increases in production, though experts from the United States mission have reported that ten thousand tons of Santa Cruz corn have been mixed into the national flour this last year, making possible a corresponding reduction in the costly import of wheat. Confident predictions have been made of cumulative increases in 1956 and 1957, in Santa Cruz and elsewhere, in the vital import crops of sugar, rice, and cotton.

Success in the development of the new area depends on the initiative that will be shown by Bolivian farmers and by the ability to attract an adequate supply of labor in what has been almost an empty region. Demand for land has been brisk, and there has been considerable spontaneous migration. Both the government and the international organizations have plans for encouraging Indians from the Altiplano and the high valleys to move to the lowlands. Four hundred colonists from Okinawa have recently been settled with United States aid, and there has also been discussion of the possibility of immigration from Europe.

Progress also depends on the development of plants for the processing of agricultural products. The government's new sugar mill will begin operations in 1956 or 1957, quadrupling the present small capacity of the industry. The intention is to arrange for private management and operation. A powdered milk plant is being built at Cochabamba with aid from UNICEF — the International Children's Fund — and from the United States. Private capital has recently established several meat-packing plants on the plains of the Beni in the northeastern part of the country. Though Bolivians fully realize that their nation has no prospects for massive industrialization, their program of diversification will not be fully successful unless private enterprise seizes the opportunities for a modest development of manufacturing based mainly on local materials.

Farming on the new frontier shows promising beginnings and should stimulate the growth of processing establishments. So far, however, the one economic success story is that of oil. Petroleum production had never approached the country's consumption needs, which had risen from three thousand to four or five thousand barrels a day. During the second half of 1952, production had fallen to about one thousand barrels a day. It has now risen to twelve thousand barrels, and observers are confident that the figure can be brought to eighteen thousand with improved arrangements for distribution. Though one private operator from the United States has begun producing under the industry's new "open-door" policy, substantially the whole of the increase has been from the fields of the State Petroleum Agency. It is primarily the result of the purchase in 1953 of three new rotary rigs and the equipment for drilling some twenty wells. This development has already shifted Bolivia from the position of an importer of oil to that of a net exporter, with Argentina and Brazil as eager customers and with the possibility of exports to Chile and the Pacific if a pipeline can be built to the coast. The government has predicted petroleum exports in 1955 of $6,000,000 as compared to imports in recent years of the same or higher figures.

Clearly, there is no easy way of summarizing the effect of these various changes. If the government enjoyed good fortune with its oil wells — and showed enterprise and determination in working them —

it confronted ill fortune in the break in the price of tin. The mining industry avoided the disaster that many observers predicted, but its operation and administration are far from satisfactory. The deficit of the *Corporación Minera* throws a burden on the national budget and contributes to an inflation which, though checked in 1953, is now rampant again. Though the new efforts in lowland agriculture show definite promise, it remains true that so far the nation's foreign payments can be balanced only by aid from the United States. Yet to a number of thoughtful observers, the problem of Bolivia appears as a race against time until the program of diversification can show its full effects.

The great transformation attempted in Bolivia is only in its early stages. The results remain uncertain and the judgments must still remain tentative. This is particularly true of the measures of land reform, in which the Bolivian government is risking the greatest break with the past.

* * *

"*El Indio nos ha servido hace cuatro siglos.* (The Indian has served us for four centuries.) Let us devote the next fifty years to serving him." So read one of the posters issued by the Bolivian government at the time of the reform. The first half of the statement was literal truth. The second half was sentimental exaggeration. But the fact that it could be said at all is an indication of the abruptness of the break with the past. The agrarian reform took power from the leading class in the community and offered a share in power to a submerged people. In the months just preceding the signature of the decree, there were plots and threats of counterrevolution; and there were cases of attacks by Indian bands on villages in the Cochabamba Valley, with deaths on both sides. Some observers even feared the outbreak of a general race war. The fact that this did not occur and that the change took place without major violence should not obscure its significance as a social transformation.

Of this, one symbol was to be found in the great parades of Indians through the streets of La Paz organized by the government in celebration of each of its many political holidays. Before the revolution, Indian men in ragged clothing used to be seen mainly in the back streets of the city or perhaps driving herds of llamas to the town houses of their patrons loaded with llama dung fuel. Now they appeared by tens of thousands marching through the main streets, many wearing traditional costumes of great variety, some bearing — though fortunately not using — their new arms, with bands playing the panpipes and other native instruments, on their way to be received by the President from the balcony of the *Palacio* or filling the stadium to hear him report on the work of the government. These were of course acts of showmanship and propaganda, largely organized by Sr. Nuflo Chávez, the Minister of the new department devoted to the *campesinos'* affairs; but they were signs of a real change of status.

It is by no means certain what kind of leadership will emerge from the ranks of the Indian population, but so far the Indians, in spite of their traditional aloofness, seem to be demonstrating political loyalty to the regime which has placed them in this new position. Certainly this is the impression received by foreign observers, including prominent figures in political life in the United States, who have had the opportunity of traveling with President Paz Estenssoro on tours of the country regions. They entered village after village through triumphal arches decorated with paper streamers, finely woven textiles, and pieces of antique silver. At each stop they were showered with confetti, and in every village they watched the President surrounded by crowds of Indians and exchanging with them hearty *abrazos*. In November 1953, a small group of ex-officers gained possession of Cochabamba and raised the banner of counterrevolution. They were quickly put down by the workers of the petroleum refinery and the landworkers from the nearest villages. A pilot who flew his plane into the Cochabamba Valley that day reported that the roads were black with *campesinos* on their way to the city to defend what they had come to believe was their revolution.

If these first indications are borne out, it would appear that the victory of the M.N.R. has changed the necessary conditions for making revolutions in a country in which they have been so common. Traditionally it has been possible for a small group of officers and leading citizens to overthrow another similar group by winning over part of the army and by staging a coup d'état — violent or bloodless — that ended with possession of the Presidential Palace and the city of La Paz. Now, for better or worse, overthrow of a government would be a more difficult business. The army alone could hardly do it, and capture of the Palace would no longer be decisive. Success of a revolt would depend on winning the support or overcoming the opposition of considerable groups in the population — certainly of the miners and the urban middle and working classes that bore arms in the uprising of 1952 and now, it would appear, of many of the Indians of the land as well. One aspect of the transformation is a broadening of the political base.

Consideration of the Bolivian experience necessarily raises the general question of the relation between revolution and economic development in countries in which the institutional pattern is unfavorable to enterprise and a productive technology. In such countries, can economic progress be advanced by revolution? The dangers, the cost, and the disadvantages of this method are obvious. They are abundantly illustrated in the Bolivian case. Revolutionary nationalization of the mines deprived the country of the services of badly needed technicians from abroad and required the government to assume administrative responsibilities which it is finding difficult to discharge. The agrarian reform imposes administrative problems of even greater complexity and puts much of the agricultural wealth of the country into the untried hands of the Indian. It risked alienation of the local class which possessed the greatest number of men of education, many of whom are now in exile. The two acts of expropriation could not fail, at least in the short run, to discourage private investment from abroad and even from within the country. Meanwhile the revolution put greater political power into the hands of those groups whose demands for higher living standards — and whose urgent needs — might become obstacles to the possibilities of further advance.

Yet, in a country like Bolivia, the opposite question may be posed with equal force. Is economic progress possible by any method other than revolution? Are any means less brusque likely to accomplish the necessary changes? Could the existing inertia have been overcome without such a revolutionary process as that initiated by the M.N.R.? Certainly there were few signs that promised fruitful evolutionary changes in the Bolivia of early 1952.[4] The economy was characterized by a dangerous reliance on monoproduction, by an archaic system of agriculture, and by a diversion of enterprise and investment into lines that made little contribution to development. Leaders of the *Movimiento* insisted that Bolivia could be broken out of the economy of a mining camp only by breaking the power of the great tin companies and that the power of the great landowners had to be broken in order to open the way for the more progressive development of the nation's agricultural resources. Certainly the regime has approached the problem of diversification with new vigor, as the United States government has recognized. It has managed in a time of great difficulty — though with outside aid — to make productive investments. The prospects remain uncertain and the perils are great.

[4] The requests and arrangements for United Nations technical assistance were, however, an indication of concern over the nation's problems.

Yet it may well be the verdict of history that this was a case in which a nationalist revolution was needed to accomplish the release and redirection of the nation's energies.

If this should include success in the release and creative development of the abilities and the energies of the long-suppressed and long-isolated Indian majority, the achievement would be very great indeed. At the beginning of these lectures, I referred to the contrast between two groups of new countries — those which began as British colonies in almost empty areas, like the United States and Australia, and those like Bolivia which began as Spanish colonies in areas of large and established Indian populations. The first group of countries have in general attained the highest standards of living in the world. They did not gain wealth as rapidly as some of the other group — unlike Bolivia they had no Potosí — but they possessed great long-run advantages. The ratio between population and resources was favorable. They had contact with the countries in which enterprise and technology were advancing more rapidly, and they took active part in that advance. Education became universal, and the working populations could successfully claim a large share of the nation's wealth. The countries of the second group, on the other hand, have been outside the main currents of economic progress, and their cultures have given greater emphasis to other values. Their economies have been characterized by poverty and extreme inequality, and their populations have been divided by the lasting cleavage between European and Indian. Now these nations, like so many others throughout the world, are setting for themselves the ideal of economic development. If they succeed in increasing productivity and in spreading its benefits throughout the whole of their long-divided populations, they will have accomplished a task in many respects more difficult than was that of the economic development of the United States.

A Mexican scholar has described Spanish humanism in the early days of the colonies as "enfolding the American Indians in its optimism."[5] After four centuries of relationships based on a different spirit, the Bolivian government is now incorporating the Andean Indian in its bold and optimistic projects of economic reform. Neither the United States nor Australia attempted, or had to attempt, so profound a change in the conditions of life of an indigenous people. It is because so much is risked and so much ventured that I ask your sympathetic and critical consideration of the current economic and social transformation of Bolivia.

[5] Silvio Zavala, *New Viewpoints on the Spanish Colonization of America* (Philadelphia, 1943), p. 113.

CELSO FURTADO

Brazil: What Kind of Revolution?*

BRAZILIANS are now widely conscious that their country is on the march toward transformations in its economic and social structure. They want to understand what is happening so that they can take intelligent positions on the issues involved. Those who must make decisions of major importance therefore owe it to the public to define their aims clearly and disclose the methods to be used in achieving them. What follows is an attempt to satisfy this requirement.

The first question often raised concerns the disproportionate social costs of the notable economic development that has been taking place in Brazil over the past several years. Economic analysis deals exclusively with the cold description of reality. We know that this development of which we are so proud has brought about no change at all in the living conditions of three-fourths of the country's population. Its main feature has been a growing concentration of income, both socially and geographically. The large mass of people who toil in the fields and constitute the majority of the Brazilian population have reaped no benefit. Worse than that, the masses have witnessed a relative decline in their standard of living as compared to those engaged in commerce and other services. As for the industrial workers, who represent a sort of middle class in the Brazilian social framework, they have grown both in absolute and relative terms, without having improved their standard of living to any large extent. They, too, have suffered a relative worsening of their economic position as compared to higher income groups employed in urban services.

It is not only in the concentration of income that economic development has produced social results of an extremely negative character. Because of the anachronistic structure of Brazilian agriculture, it has led in many regions to a relative increase in the rent from land, thus rewarding parasitic groups. Similarly, in the absence

* *Foreign Affairs,* vol. 41 #3 (April 1963); copyright by the Council on Foreign Relations, Inc., New York. Reprinted by permission of *Foreign Affairs* and the Council on Foreign Relations, Inc.

of a conscious policy designed to further the social purposes of state action, a variety of subsidies have been improvised, which — in the name of development — have very often put a premium on investments which either were superfluous or fostered a still greater concentration of income in the hands of privileged groups. Through capital contributions, such as subsidized exchange and credit, large amounts of social wealth have been transferred to a few hands.

In political and administrative fields the distortions are still more glaring. The expansion and diversification of state functions — both as cause and effect of the development — have not been followed up by the necessary basic reforms within the state structure, and as a result waste in public administration has enormously increased. This, combined with the state's increased role in the field of investments, has created ideal conditions for the illicit acquisition of capital at the people's expense. Big contracts for public works have become the current source for amassing fortunes both within and without the government.

The resulting popular indignation, especially among the young, is easily understood. People see their supposed representatives being elected through the influence of contract-mongers for public works; they see an alliance between operators of the feudal machine and those who make budgetary appropriations resulting in the election to Congress of legislators who know they will survive politically only if they remain docile stooges in the hands of their financial patrons.

Some might object that things were much worse before; elections then were a mere formality, since an oligarchy decided for itself what would be called the will of the people. But the objection is no longer valid. If we know where the failings of the system lie — and we do — then we are able to change them; if we do not try to do so, we will be conniving with them.

There is also the other side — the positive gains of development. It has provided the country with the instruments to make decisions, given it the ability to exercise choice and, by making the people conscious of their destiny, has made them responsible for their own failings. The root cause of the present state of uneasiness in Brazil is this simple truth: we know where the errors of our development lie, and we know that it is within our power to eradicate or minimize them.

II

The second point which I would like to elaborate is the need for a philosophy to guide our action. Many people both in Brazil and abroad have asked me why Marxism has permeated Brazilian youth so deeply. The reason is simple: Marxism, in any of its varieties, affords a diagnosis of the social reality and a guide to action. We must approach this subject with absolute frankness if we are to maintain an effective dialogue with the idealistic and active youth of our time. What does their Marxism consist of?

It may be summed up by describing a few of their attitudes. They maintain: (1) that the present social order is based to a great extent on the exploitation of man by man, which favors the well-being of a class sheltering many a parasite and idler and leaves the great majority in poverty; (2) that the social reality is *historical* and thus in permanent change; therefore the present order must be superseded by another; and (3) that it is possible to identify the strategic factors which affect the social process; this in turn opens the way to a conscious policy of social reconstruction.

If we go deep into the core of this philosophy, we shall find on the one hand the wish to liberate man from all chains that socially enslave him, allowing him to fulfill his potentialities; and on the other hand an optimistic attitude concerning the capacity of human communities for self-determination. In the last analysis, what we find is a higher stage of humanism, for while it places man in the center of its concerns, it recognizes that full individual development can be attained only through a rational guidance of social relations.

Whatever name we choose to give this conception, it is impossible to object to it openly, for it is inspired by the most profound longings of modern man. It has its roots in the humanism of the Renaissance, which taught man that he could affect his own destiny; and its inherent optimism emanates from the Industrial Revolution, which gave man the power to affect his own environment.

In our dialogue with the new generation we must reach agreement as to what is really fundamental. We should relegate to the background all things that are merely instrumental or subordinate to the ends pursued. For example, it would not be possible to ascribe more than an instrumental character to the private ownership of means of production — in short, to private enterprise. We are all agreed that private enterprise is merely a decentralized form of organizing production which must be ruled by social criteria. Whenever there is a conflict between the social aims of production and its organization as a private concern, measures have to be taken to preserve the social interest. On the other hand, as a greater abundance in the supply of goods is reached, that is to say, in the higher stages of development, the actual organization of production becomes less important while the control of political power increases in importance. It is the latter, finally, that dictates the patterns of distribution and utilization of social income, in the form of either public or private consumption.

We may well ask, therefore, what are the fundamental aims on which we can unite? Should these aims be considered as ends in themselves and related to our own conception of life? It is of the highest importance, I believe, that we define these objectives clearly. Otherwise we shall not distinguish means from ends and will risk treating what others consider merely means as though they were ends. We have the right to take a stand as to the ultimate ends we are trying to attain without reference to the issue of Russian or American preëminence on the world stage. To subordinate the future of our culture to the tactical conveniences of either of the two great centers of military power would mean to give up the struggle before it is joined. We must consider the Russian-American stalemate as a given fact of the present day. By doing this we admit that it is not in our power to change the balance of forces to any significant degree. Our very helplessness regarding the world conflict gives us a wider margin of liberty to establish our own aims. And, as often happens, greater freedom gives rise to greater awareness of responsibility.

It is against this background that we must establish irrevocable aims of political action. I believe that they can be described as humanism and optimism concerning the material development of society. Or, to use more current terms, liberty and economic development.

I have used the word humanism because liberty can also be understood in terms of nineteenth-century individualism, which often saw the individual as opposed to society. There is not the slightest doubt that aspirations of our present-day youth center about authentic humanism. What makes them angry is the inhuman aspect of our development — the growing contrast between wasteful wealth and abject poverty. They see peasants living in the country but unable to grow enough food and suffering hunger almost every day of the year. They see state capitals where 10 percent of the population are listed in hospital registries as suffering from tuberculosis. And we know that all this can be remedied, indeed has already disappeared from a large portion of the world. We can see then that what worries youth is man and his degradation, and the consciousness that we are also responsible for it.

III

Once we have defined our aims, the question is how to pull ourselves together to achieve them. How can we prevent the struggle for intermediate or secondary objectives from making us forget our authentic ends? It is an extremely difficult problem, especially as the historical experience of recent decades has suggested that the underdeveloped countries must make a choice between individual liberty and rapid material development. This false dilemma is posed both by the champions of liberty and by the promoters of mass welfare.

It is now clear that the rapid material development of the Soviet Union, until recently an underdeveloped country, was achieved partly by the use of inhuman methods. The requisitioning of agricultural surpluses in order to finance industrial development was accomplished by the use of armed force, through compulsory collectivization and the violent suppression of all resistance. In order to justify these drastic methods, the "theory" was put forward that the peasant was fundamentally an individualist and that the only way to overcome such "individualism" was by enforced collectivization. This is the theory of salvation through punishment. To achieve administrative efficiency an enormous price was paid in human lives. But even if we put aside the painful Soviet experience, account must be taken of the evidence that the rapid economic development of the Communist countries has been achieved under forms of socio-political organization in which individual liberty was restricted beyond the limits which we would consider tolerable.

It must be recognized, however, that the masses in the underdeveloped countries have not generally put the same high valuation on individual liberty that we do. Since they have not had access to the better things of life, they obviously cannot grasp the full meaning of the supposed dilemma between liberty and quick development. Also, if we were to assert that rapid economic development of socialist countries was achieved only at the price of restricting civil liberties, we must then accept the corollary that the liberty enjoyed by the minority in our society is paid for by a delay in general economic development, hence is at the expense of the welfare of the great majority.

Even less effective with the peasant is the argument that the development of the socialist countries is being obtained at an enormous human cost, including forms of semi-slave labor. The fact is that the underdeveloped peoples are quite prepared to pay a price, even a very heavy one, for their development. They know by hard experience the extremely high price they pay for remaining underdeveloped. How many millions of lives are sacrificed every year in a country like Brazil by underdevelopment? How many millions of lives are lost through hunger and physical exhaustion? How many millions of human beings live without access to primary education, or any opportunity of sharing in secondary and higher education? Very few of us have sufficient awareness of these deeply inhuman characteristics of underdevelopment. When we do become fully aware, we understand why the masses are prepared for any sacrifice in order to overcome it. If the price of liberty for the few had to be the poverty of the many, we can be quite certain that the probability of preserving freedom would be practically nil.

Insistence on false alternatives nevertheless goes on, elaborated in different forms by opposing champions. The self-appointed defenders of liberty argue that the structural changes in the social order necessary for the rapid acceleration of economic development have always been associated with the suppression of fundamental human liberties. Those who take the opposite side argue from the historical fact that the only effective method for introducing the social changes necessary for rapid development has been a revolution of the Marxist-Leninist type, which by its own nature requires the setting up of a rigid dictatorship. So both sides acknowledge that social change is the effective instrument for accelerating material development in underdeveloped countries.

The discussion of this very important point has been bedevilled by a great confusion of ideas, either unconscious or deliberate. We should not forget that the method of Marxism-Leninism was created and perfected in the struggle for the overthrow of an entirely rigid socio-political structure — that of tsarism. The historical experience of the last decades has shown that such a revolutionary technique applied against other rigid structures — Nationalist China, Japanese-occupied China and Batista's Cuba are obvious examples — can be highly effective where accompanied by a Spartan discipline in the rank and file and the daring of an Alexander in the leadership.

The same does not apply, however, to "open" societies. The example of Western Europe seems conclusive: Huge party machines guided by Marxism-Leninism found themselves bewildered by an ever changing socio-political reality. This was because Marxism-Leninism sees in the state — which it defines as "a special repressive force" — the dictatorship of a class, the bourgeoisie. From the moment the state ceases to be the mere dictatorship of a class to become a composite system, though under the aegis of a certain class, the unity of revolutionary action is weakened by an inability any longer to define the party's aims. The need to discriminate between good and bad policies of the state requires a capacity for adaptation that a monolithic revolutionary party cannot have.

We cannot, then, ignore the historical fact that the Marxist-

Leninist techniques have been proved ineffective in dealing with open societies. Nor can we escape the following conclusions: (1) that dictatorships were not created by the acceleration of development but preceded it; (2) that the acceleration took place only in structures which were previously rigid (dictatorships); and (3) that the techniques which have so far been used for the rapid transformation of social structures have been effective only in rigid societies (dictatorships).

So the fundamental problem we face is to develop techniques which will make rapid social transformations possible, while retaining the pattern of an open society.

Before turning to specifically Brazilian questions, I will indulge in one more observation on revolutionary methods: Since Marxism-Leninism is based on the substitution of the dictatorship of one class for that of another class, it would be politically retrogressive to apply it to societies which have attained more complex social forms — that is, modern open societies. It would mean, in the last resort, a sacrifice of the very objectives previously described as essential. While it is true that economic development means a fuller life for man, it is no less true that the pattern of social and political organization is the warp that sustains the woof of a fuller and richer life. Although it is probable that in the future material abundance will coexist with forms of socio-political organization which permit the full realization of authentic human values, that does not necessarily occur at the present historical stage. To have attained higher forms of social and political organization is at least as great an achievement as that of high standards of material development.

Historical experience has demonstrated that whenever a revolution of the Marxist-Leninist type has been imposed on a complex social structure — as in the case of certain European countries — socialism as a form of humanism becomes perverted. As there is no possibility of converting an open society into a dictatorship without creating a climate of frustration, there is a deterioration of social values. Since the dictatorial régime does not permit the individual to play his proper part in society, a series of social myths is put forward in order to replace genuine human values. Thus, material development can take place at the same time that the dictatorship is consolidating itself upon principles which are the antithesis of humanistic revolutionary ideals.

IV

Let us now face up to the Brazilian problem. The fact is that our society is an "open" one to the industrial workers, but not to the peasants. It is therefore not hard to explain why the peasant is much more susceptible to revolutionary techniques of the Marxist-Leninist type than is the industrial working class, although from the orthodox Marxist point of view the latter should be the vanguard of the revolutionary movement. But our political system allows the urban workers to organize themselves in order to press their claims, within the rules of the democratic game, whereas the situation of the peasants is altogether different. Since they have no rights, they cannot have legal claims. If they organize themselves, the inference is that they do so for subversive purposes. The necessary conclusion we must draw is that Brazilian society is rigid at least in that large sector composed of agricultural laborers. As regards this sector, we have to accept the fact that the Marxist-Leninist revolutionary techniques are effective.

We come now to a conclusion of great importance in Brazil. To the extent that we live in an open society, the attainment of higher social aims tends to assume the form of gradualism. To the extent that we live in a rigid society, those objectives will tend to be attained by cataclysmic disruption. Thus there is a duality within the Brazilian revolutionary process.

What is the likelihood of an effective Brazilian revolution through Marxist-Leninist methods? I believe there are two ways in which this might occur. As suggested above, the first one is connected with the land problem. We must not forget that over half of the Brazilian population gets its living from the land. If this sector maintains its present rigidity, every peasant movement will tend rapidly to adopt revolutionary techniques of the Marxist-Leninist type. Thus we have an important segment of the population with a Marxist-Leninist bias which, given certain conditions, might be able to take the lead in the Brazilian revolutionary process. The practical results would be the predominance of the least developed sector of our society. The real objectives of our development, as previously defined in terms of humanism, would thus be partially frustrated at the very start.

The second way in which a revolution of the Marxist-Leninist type might be carried out would be as a result of social and political retrogression. We have observed that a revolution of this type is hardly likely in an open society, unless it is imposed from without, as happened in some countries of Central Europe. Nevertheless, the possibility of "putting the clock back" must not be excluded. The imposition of a right-wing dictatorship, making the whole political structure rigid, would create favorable conditions for an effective revolution of the Marxist-Leninist type. But even in this case, the agrarian sector would be likely to predominate. In the absence of conditions resulting from political retrogression, the only possibility of a Marxist-Leninist revolution lies in the persistence of an archaic agrarian structure.

In order to achieve a high rate of economic development, in accordance with truly social criteria, we shall have to bring about some important changes in our basic structures. Because we have not been prepared for such changes, anxiety has grown from day to day. We have come to live in what may properly be termed a pre-revolutionary period, in which drastic change is a political necessity. Thus techniques of social transformation and revolutionary methods are in the forefront of present-day political concern. If we are to avoid dictatorial régimes, whether of a social class or ideological group or rigid party machine, we must: (a) prevent all forms of retrogression in our social and political systems; and (b) create conditions for fast and effective change in the country's archaic agrarian structure.

These general directives must be elaborated into specific lines of action. Political retrogression will not come haphazardly, but as a reflection of panic among some priviliged groups confronted with growing social pressure. Where structures are rigid, preventing gradual adaptations, these pressures may create cataclysmic situations, leading to emergency solutions or preventive coups. Thus, the first task is to give more flexibility to the existing structures. We have to tread boldly the path of constitutional change which will permit agrarian reform and a radical change of government administration of the fiscal system and the banking structure. We have to subordinate state action to a clear definition of the aims of economic and social development. The Congress has the right to draw up directives, but local politicians must be deprived of the power to allocate public moneys. We have to give the government effective means to punish those who embezzle public funds, to control extravagant consumption and to dignify the function of civil servants. We must have legal statutes to subordinate the action of foreign capital to the aims of economic development and to the requirements of political independence. The recent law affecting the remittance of profits constitutes a clear indication that, even in a legislature where conservative views prevail, there is an awareness of a need for such discipline. Passed at a moment of serious political tension, the law contains ambiguities and, therefore, ought to be improved. It is taken for granted that the coöperation of foreign capital is indispensable for the development of any underdeveloped country; but in the absence of regulation, conflicts of economic interest may become conflicts of a political nature, harmful to international coöperation. Also, the government must have thorough knowledge of the sources of all investment in means of mass communications. And above all we must have a plan for economic and social development compatible with our own possibilities and in conformity with the aspirations of the people.

What must we do to translate into action all these objectives? I believe that the most immediate task is to organize public opinion so that it can express itself. It is up to the students, workers, entrepreneurs, intellectuals and perhaps even the peasants, through their incipient organizations, to start a frank debate about what they expect from their government. The more complex problems must be given systematic study by groups of specialists, and their conclusions must be publicly debated. Brazil is mature enough to start thinking about its own destiny. From general debates and from expressions of public opinion must emerge programs that will serve as a basis for the renewal of popular representation.

EDMUNDO FLORES

Land Reform and the Alliance for Progress*

UNLESS President Kennedy and his advisors are willing to accept the necessity for drastic — and sometimes violent — revolutionary change in Latin America, his ambitious Alliance for Progress will fail, no matter how many billions of dollars the United States is willing to spend on it. This may seem an extreme view, but — as the operation of the Alliance has already shown in the one year since its birth — it presents no more than the hard reality that Americans will have to face.

* Woodrow Wilson School of Public and International Affairs, Center of International Studies, *Policy Memorandum #27* (May 1963). Reprinted by permission of the author and of the Center of International Studies.

The most striking feature of Latin America today is a pervasive urge for economic, social, and political change. Attempts to stifle this drive will only create more powerful tensions. The fact is that the archaic institutions of Latin America are doomed and will soon disintegrate — one by one. Whether this process will occur in an orderly fashion seems a rather naive query. Anyone acquainted with Latin American politics knows there is, on all sides, a deeply ingrained and rather trigger-happy inclination to resolve political conflicts by the use of force. Undoubtedly the coming revolution will have elements of violence. One need only remember that the casualties of the Mexican Revolution of 1910 approached one million, or that the ten-year-old guerrilla warfare currently going on in the backlands of Colombia reportedly has cost 300,000 lives. Figures on casualties in Cuba, before and after Castro, in the Dominican Republic, Haiti, or Guatemala are undisclosed but must be very high, too.

The critical question, I think, is whether the drive for change will be repressed, leading to a deadlock and turning Latin America into an active international battlefield in the cold war; or whether this drive will be confined to internal conflict, leaving it enough vitality to create a more suitable framework for general development.

One of the harsh facts of political life in Latin America has been that would-be reformers have faced the determined opposition of the landed elite, the armed forces, and the Catholic Church, as well as (except during the Good Neighbor days) the almost inevitable and generally decisive interference of the United States on the side of all three. Considering that they had such formidable opponents, the number of successful revolutions is impressive: Mexico, Bolivia, and Cuba. Behind these movements was the gathering momentum of what is nowadays called the "revolution of rising expectations."

The increasing demand of the masses for social change and rapid economic improvement can be attributed only in part to overt propaganda. I find, for instance, that the impact of professional agencies like the Communist Party, the Voice of America, the various organs of the United Nations, and local political parties is overrated. Largely speaking, their output is either incomprehensible or dull. In contrast, the impression made by the Mexican, Bolivian, and Cuban revolutions is much deeper. And no one has fully gauged the powerful impact of American movies which have displayed the standard of living in the United States to Latin American workers.

I remember witnessing near-riots in the movie houses of small villages in the Andean plateau — where I worked for the United Nations as a land reform expert for almost three years — every time the picture of Zapata, Mexico's legendary agrarian leader, appeared on the screen. It was strange to hear the peasant crowds shouting the old Mexican slogans: Viva Zapata! Land and Freedom! Death to the landlords!

For many years now the principal market for Mexican movies has been rural South America. Here, the supremacy of Mexican films is unchallenged — not because they are particularly good, but because peasants are illiterate and these pictures are in Spanish. The exploits of Zapata, Villa, Cantinflas — the pathetic, rebellious outcast — and of the anonymous heroines portrayed by Dolores del Rio, convey more of a message than, say, the Communist Manifesto ever has. In 1952, the news spread, by word of mouth, all over neighboring countries, that the new revolutionary government was giving the Bolivian Indians their own land. Recently, particularly after the Bay of Pigs incident, the popularity of Castro has skyrocketed — regardless of what Latin American diplomats may say.

Thus political change comes about not only from the interplay of economic forces and the push of ideologies but also from the massive unleashing of what economists call "demonstration effects"—the growing awareness of new and appealing patterns of consumption and leisure popularized by the media of mass communication: movies, commercial advertising, tourism, etc. In advanced countries such demonstration effects act together with rising levels of income and employment to change consumers' preferences and to stimulate the economy. In underdeveloped countries, where the income levels of the masses tend to be static or deteriorating and unemployment is chronic, such effects are explosive because they exacerbate deep-seated frustration.

If the Alliance for Progress is going to work at all, it must confront these enormous forces of active discontent which are growing at a pace that would shock most North Americans if they knew about them.

Fidel Castro has claimed to be the indirect promoter of the *Alianza;* and there is some truth in his boast, since without the Cuban Revolution Latin America would not be in the headlines today — except for its normal quota of earthquakes, air crashes, political assassinations, and assorted folklore. Without Castro, few outside Latin America would care about the region's economic stagnation, its political instability, or its undeniable ability to upset the balance of power in the cold war.

Regardless of Castro's claims, the Kennedy Administration has taken up the challenge of helping to develop this vast continent.

But the Alliance for Progress is a more difficult and ambitious undertaking than the Marshall Plan. While the Marshall Plan financed the reconstruction of war-torn but highly advanced industrial societies, the Alliance requires no less than the complete transmutation of old, stagnant, and deeply divided societies into new, unified, and dynamic ones.

So far, besides taking a political gamble, the United States government has advanced its first cash installment and has made the initial moves to organize the administrative and technical machinery in charge of implementing the program. In long-run terms, the United States has promised 20 billion dollars over ten years to finance development. It has also made clear to the Latin American governments that aid will not be granted unless they put into effect land reform and progressive taxation programs.

The need for policies that will redistribute land and wealth in order to start economic development is generally accepted among economists. For instance, W. W. Rostow has suggested that, above minimum levels of consumption, income that is "largely concentrated in the hands of those who own land, must be shifted into the hands of those who will spend it on roads and railroads, schools and factories rather than on country houses and servants, personal ornaments and temples."[1]

Thus the emphasis of the *Alianza* on redistributive policies appears to be correct. Unfortunately, it will be extremely difficult to accomplish. In advanced countries, income redistribution can be achieved with relative ease by resorting to progressive taxation, but in less-developed areas such is not the case. In their present stage of development, most Latin American countries cannot apply progressive income taxation for several reasons. First, the really powerful people in most of these countries do not want it, since it would be tantamount to abdicating their power. Second, underdevelopment itself precludes the possibility of efficient taxation because, for one thing, all major as well as minor appointments are political and there is hence no effective civil service to carry it out. For another, administrative corruption prevails throughout the Latin American governments that are dominated by tiny minorities of the rich, and there is a long-standing tradition of tax evasion.

It should be understood that, with the possible exceptions of Argentina, Brazil, Chile, Costa Rica, Mexico, and Uruguay, there

[1] W. W. Rostow, *The Stages of Economic Growth* (Cambridge, England: University Press, 1960), p. 19.

are no appreciable middle classes in Latin America and consequently there is a desperate shortage of trained personnel on the lower levels. It may not be difficult to find aggressive lawyers, cultured priests, chivalrous soldiers, and even good doctors. But trained nurses, moderately efficient stenographers, or reliable proofreaders are terribly scarce even in the more advanced countries. The rigid social structure, the lack of employment opportunities, and a tradition which equates leisure with a high social status have prevented the emergence of this new class in either industry, commerce, or the bureaucracy.

Thus political opposition, administrative corruption, and the shortage of trained personnel on the lower levels create a vicious circle which can only be eliminated in the long run. For instance, take the experience of Mexico after the Revolution. Even under a regime for which the organization of a moderately efficient civil service was a matter of survival, this process has taken close to four decades and it is still open to substantial improvement. It is true that while in 1924 income taxes accounted for 1 per cent of total revenue, in 1960 they had climbed to 34 per cent. But although these figures reflect progress, taxation is still fairly regressive and — despite vigorous efforts of the present administration — in all probability it will take from ten to twenty years to perfect the tax system of Mexico.

In conclusion, as many Latin American experts on taxation well know, the political and administrative backwardness characteristic of most Latin American countries makes it virtually impossible to redistribute income by progressive taxation in the immediate future; and even under the most favorable circumstances, including outside incentives, it will take years to correct this situation. Therefore, one of the requirements of the present *Alianza* policy does not prevail.

The situation is little better when it comes to the chances of land reform. In this case there are precedents from which we can draw valuable lessons. In fact, most Latin American countries have land reform legislation of sorts, but they have never applied it on a significant scale. So far only four countries — Mexico, Bolivia, Guatemala, and Cuba — have embarked on substantial land reform; and of these, the Cuban experience is too recent to allow sound comment. The Guatemalan reform launched in 1952 was soon aborted, through efforts abetted by the U. S. government. Generalization from the Bolivian case is premature although this reform started ten years ago. The only clear case is provided by Mexico's reform, initiated 45 years ago after seven years of civil war.

The common characteristic of the four cases is that they were preceded by violent revolution and brought about the virtual destruction of the political and economic power of the landed classes. In the case of Guatemala, however, American intervention restored to power the old landed elite, and in the process managed to create one of the most incompetent, embarrassing, and irresponsible governments of Latin America.

Since in underdeveloped countries the main sources of wealth are land and mineral resources, it is obvious that their pattern of income distribution is ultimately determined by the pattern of land and mineral ownership. Therefore, the income shifts required for development must necessarily take place in these economic areas. Although technically the differences between a mineral-exporting economy and an agrarian economy are considerable, there are also important similarities. As Professor Raymond J. Penn put it bluntly, "U. S. industry cannot operate in a feudal country without accepting the rules of feudalism and thus sharing the villain's role for those who want to strengthen the economic and legal position of the landless and jobless."[2] There is no doubt that this unfortunate symbiosis will complicate tremendously the launching of land reforms in Latin America.

In Mexico and Bolivia before their agrarian reforms, approximately 3 per cent of the population owned 90 per cent of the productive land; that meant that a correspondingly large proportion of *agricultural cash income* accrued to only a tiny proportion of the total population. Such a high concentration of land ownership and agricultural income prevails today in many Latin American countries and this explains precisely why such countries have lacked development.

Briefly outlined, the most important results of Mexico's land reform have been as follows:

From 1915 to date, 108 million acres of all types of land — more than 50 per cent of all the productive land of the country — have been distributed among 2 million peasants. These lands were freely granted to agricultural communities called *ejidos*. The *ejido* is a system of communal tenure modeled after the ancient Indian communities whose land was usurped by the *hacienda*. *Ejido* lands are held as the property of a town or a village either for collective use or for distribution among *ejidatarios* for cultivation in small plots to which each individual has a right of occupancy and usufruct. The average size of these plots is 16 acres. *Ejido* lands cannot be sold or mort gaged. At present there are 18,000 *ejidos;* of these, approximately 4,000 are operated collectively and produce cotton, sugar cane, rice, and hemp. The remaining 14,000 are operated individually.

The Mexican land reform also created small family farms called *pequenas propiedades.* These units were inspired by the American family farm. Their area varies from 250 to 350 acres of irrigated land or its equivalent in land of lower quality. These farms were created from lands which were exempt from expropriation when the *ejidos* were formed and remained the private property of the former *hacienda* owners.

At present there are approximately 40,000 *pequenas propiedades* with an average size of between 250 and 600 acres which cover an area of around 17 million acres of the best land. In addition, there are more than a million privately owned holdings of smaller size and, finally, there still remain some 500 *haciendas* of between 125,000 and 250,000 acres each. As a rule, these *haciendas* are located in remote semi-desert regions or in tropical jungles, or else they are owned by powerful politicians.

The transformation of land ownership in Mexico could not be more dramatic. Before the land reform there were 8,400 very large *haciendas* and 48,600 medium-sized and small plots, making a grand total of 57,000 properties. Today, there are 2.7 million holdings. Half of the productive land was granted to 2 million *ejidatarios* (1.3 million holdings operated individually and collectively); the other half belongs to approximately 1.4 million private farmers.

With the land reform it became imperative to increase productivity, to diversify production, and to industrialize. Since 1930, the agricultural product has increased at an average annual rate of 5.4 per cent, while gross national product increased at a rate of 6.2 per cent annually. Cotton production increased 17 times; coffee 8 times; beans 6 times; tomatoes and wheat 4 times; sugar cane 2.5 times; corn production doubled. On the industrial front, steel output increased 14 times, from 102,800 metric tons in 1930 to 1.6 million tons in 1960; generation of electricity went up 5.6 times, from 1.4 million KWH in 1930 to 9.8 million in 1960; cement output increased 12.7 times, from 224,000 metric tons to 3.1 million in 1960; petroleum is up from 106,351 barrels a day in 1938 — when Mexico expropriated foreign oil holdings — to 320,070 barrels a day in 1961. The final payment for expropriated oil holdings was made in the fall of 1962.

Meanwhile the population rose from 15 million before the Revolution to 36 million today. In 1910, 90 per cent of the total labor force was engaged in farming; today only 50 per cent are farmers and the rest have shifted to newly created urban-industrial jobs or have joined the ranks of the unemployed. Despite rapid industrialization, Mexico has not been able to create enough new jobs each year and unemployment is its most severe problem.

Undoubtedly the break-up of the *hacienda* was the catalyst which released and set in motion the multitude of complex forces to which Mexico owes its sustained rates of agricultural and industrial growth. It gave the rural population an opportunity for both horizontal and vertical mobility; it destroyed the "caste" system, it profoundly affected the political environment and brought the country out of the colonial impasse; it opened it up to technological progress and paved the way for the beginning of road building and irrigation programs. Urban expansion and the public works policy created a huge demand for cement, steel, and other products of the construction industry, thus setting the basis for Mexico's industrial revolution.

Land reform gave Mexico a government with a new concern for the people and the nation. It did something more. It gave to many of the common people something they had never had: the idea of progress and personal ambition for a better future for their children.

Without the agrarian revolution, Mexico would probably be today in a situation similar to that of contemporary Colombia, Peru, or Venezuela. There would be good roads leading from ports to mines, oil wells, and plantations; industry and farming would show development along a few specific lines. One would find urban expansion, Hilton hotels, air-conditioning, supermarkets, funiculars, submarines, and other conspicuous construction. In patches, the economy would display a semblance of technological sophistication. But there would be little or no evidence of the rise of new classes that accompanied the industrial growth of the advanced nations.

Mexico avoided this chromium-plated dead-end road because, irrespective of the deficiencies of the *ejido* and of the *pequena propiedad*, massive land redistribution forced the way for concurrent social and economic improvement. Mexico's development has been so spectacular that in a recent book Eugene R. Black, President of the International Bank for Reconstruction and Development, and an acknowledged tough critic, lumps together Russia, Mexico, and Japan as countries that "have yet to achieve high consumption economies, but could conceivably achieve them in the foreseeable future."[3]

[3] *The Diplomacy of Economic Development* (Cambridge, Mass.: Harvard University Press, 1960), p. 2.

Experience indicates, therefore, that it is a serious mistake to consider land reform as merely a matter of introducing more efficient farming methods, opening new lands, and partitioning large *idle* estates. Land reform is much more than that, regardless of what influential Latin American landlords disguised as progressives may say about it, and regardless of the misleading and naive utterances occasionally emanating from Washington which describe it as a measure that is not going to hurt anybody.

Land reform should not be confused with the introduction of efficiency in farming by means of hybrid seeds, extension services, or the like. These measures, necessary as they are, do not basically alter income distribution or the social and political structure. Efforts to increase efficiency must be applied *after* land reform takes place, *not instead of it.* Producing more cotton, coffee, sugar, bananas, or even maize, without changing the structure of land tenure, will not open up new alternatives for the *hacienda* or plantation workers and probably will not even raise their level of nutrition.

Land reform should not be confused with attempts either to reclaim unproductive land or to settle in uninhabited areas. Here a word of warning seems appropriate, since some Latin American countries (Guatemala, Colombia, and Peru) already are embarking upon such a travesty under the Alliance for Progress. Opening public domain lands, before industrial development gets under way is inadvisable, because their fertility is highly questionable and the large capital outlays required can be put to better use elsewhere in the economy. We should not forget that in the course of several centuries these lands failed to tempt either the Indian farmers who preceded Columbus, the Spanish conquerors, or the Catholic Church — all of whom coveted land and knew what to do with it. The reason for such neglect is obvious: under prevailing conditions, public domain lands often are worthless because of their distance from markets and their poor fertility as well as the prevalence of bad weather and an unhealthy climate. Spending scarce capital to open up more land in underdeveloped agrarian countries is bad economics. The limiting factor for development in these countries is not lack of land, but rather the inefficient way in which it is now distributed.

Land reform in fact amounts to the adoption of a new pattern of income distribution: a capital levy on a few landlords that is distributed among many peasants and the state. This initial income shift greatly facilitates the increase of the domestic rate of capital formation, as proven spectacularly in the case of Mexico, where from 1910 to 1942 all sources of foreign capital were closed owing to widespread expropriations. Nonetheless, during this period Mexico set the basis for her industrial and agricultural expansion.

If the land is purchased — rather than expropriated — this represents not land reform but merely a real estate transaction. If proprietors receive cash compensation, there is an income redistribution effect only to the degree to which cash compensation is inferior to the price of land. If the government pays the large landowners in bonds, this in effect forces landowners to lend to the government an amount equal to the price they receive for the land.

In other words, to be effective land reform has to *take productive land* (and its income) from the landlords without immediate compensation. Otherwise it is not a redistributive measure. To pretend that landlords should be fully compensated is as absurd as to expect that taxpayers of advanced countries should receive cash compensation or bonds by an amount equal to their taxes.

In line with this principle, the four cases of land reform already attempted have shown strong confiscatory tendencies.

The Mexican government issued bond to compensate Mexican landlords, but only approximately 0.5 per cent of the total value of expropriated land was paid for. Even in the case of land owned by foreigners (79 million acres), compensation was not paid in accordance with the rigid principle of "prompt, adequate, and effective" payment as the U. S. State Department demanded. Instead, it was subject to long and protracted negotiation, culminating in an agreement between the Mexican and American governments in which payment was geared to the financial capacity of the expropriating country and extended over a long period of time.

In Bolivia, according to the land reform decree, owners of expropriated land were to be compensated with agrarian bonds, but so far only token payments have been made. The same applies to the Guatemalan and Cuban cases. It is interesting to note that although in the Mexican, Guatemalan, and Cuban reforms the American government showed a deep concern about the problem of compensation, in Bolivia it extended economic aid instead. In this case, as Professor Robert J. Alexander wrote in 1958, ". . . the United States has said to Bolivia and to the world that this country does not necessarily support the status quo in semifeudal underdeveloped nations."[4] (This may be particularly true, one is tempted to add, in cases in which there are no American investors in the countries in question.)

[4] Robert J. Alexander, *The Bolivian National Revolution* (New Brunswick, N. J.: Rutgers University Press, 1958), pp. xvii–xviii.

Perhaps the success of the *Alianza* and the survival of the U. S. investments in mining, public utilities, and other businesses in countries like Peru, Chile, and Brazil will ultimately depend upon the ability of American businessmen who operate in these countries to join the side of the groups who favor social change.

I am aware of the fact that traditionally in the United States any proposal involving confiscatory practices has awakened repugnance and has been rejected. (It might be said that one of the outstanding exceptions was the seizure of property, without compensation, represented by the 1.3 million slaves valued at $3,000 million who were freed by the Lincoln Administration.) I also know that today, in the cold war, this attitude has become even more firm — respect for private property and due process of law has come to be the signal indicator to separate those who are on the side of democracy from those who are on the Communist side.

This standard may be relevant to American domestic politics but when applied to underdeveloped countries, with entirely different traditions, it leads to what George F. Kennan, referring to past American foreign policy, has called ". . . the colossal conceit of thinking that you could suddenly make international life over into what you believed to be your own image."[5] To project, evaluate, and judge land reform against the American experience is misleading, if not meaningless. What is needed in Latin America is a program to develop a continent that never had settlers, or homesteads or farms operated by individual families, or an equalitarian democratic tradition.

Unlike the United States, many of these Latin American countries still have to overcome feudal traditions, a lack of social mobility, and economic stagnation. Much of rural Latin America is populated by the descendants of the Conquerors and of conquered Indians. There, *haciendas* and plantations often exceed hundreds of thousands of acres and are worked by peons according to ancient, rigid, and often inhuman practices. The ruling groups have never worked the land themselves. In most rural areas there is no democracy or due process of law.

As J. K. Galbraith has observed: ". . . some of our current discussion of land reform in the underdeveloped countries proceeds as though this reform were something that a government proclaims on any fine morning — that it gives land to tenants as it might give

[5] *American Diplomacy, 1900–1950* (New York: Mentor Books, 1951), p. 69.

pensions to old soldiers or as it might reform the administration of justice. In fact, a land reform is a revolutionary step; it passes power, property, and status from one group in the community to another. If the government of the country is dominated or strongly influenced by the land-holding groups — the one that is losing its prerogatives — no one should expect effective land legislation as an act of grace. . . . The best assurance of land reform, which I for one hope can be orderly and peaceful, is a popular government by those who really want reform."[6]

Viewed in its true light, land reform is a very drastic measure which crushes the power of the landed elite wherever it is applied. Landlords know this and, regardless of the lip service they pay to the *Alianza,* they will frustrate it in every possible way. It would not be surprising if they pocketed as much of the 20 billion as they can on the grounds of political self-defense. One need only remember, for instance, that food grants to Peru and other Latin American countries under the Point IV Program often failed to go to famine areas and instead were sold on the markets, and the money went into the pockets of speculators. Administrative corruption and graft is an art about which underdeveloped countries have little to learn and may even be able to teach something to developed ones.

Thus the position of the U. S. government is tragic, and perhaps absurd: it wishes to entrust what is nothing less than a revolution to the very group — the safe conservative element — which in its own interest must block it, as it always has. In other words, it is the same as if Abraham Lincoln had expected the Southern slave owners to expropriate themselves.

On the other hand, all those who are temperamentally inclined toward change as well as those who have nothing to lose by it — intellectuals, students, wishful democrats ahead of their time, landless peasants, unemployed urban workers — all these, paradoxically, are the *Alianza's* true and natural allies, provided that they are somehow able to wrest control of it from the hands of the old elite for their own benefit. These are the men and women who, given the chance, would build the schools, factories, and roads essential for economic growth.

One key question remains. What is to prevent the Communists from taking advantage of the coming revolutions to impose their control over Latin America?

---

[6] Quoted by Gunnar Myrdal in *An International Economy* (New York: Harper & Brothers, 1956), pp. 183–84.

Clearly, the time for self-deception or self-righteousness is past. Ignoring this problem would be fatal. Leaning on standard, hollow exhortations in favor of ideal democracy and free elections — so dear to the Voice of America and to American embassies — is not only futile but quite embarrassing to the Latin Americans who want to build democracy: Americans may be masters in commercial advertising but in political propaganda their efforts tend to be inept and ineffective. Subsidizing and arming the anti-revolutionary and dictatorial groups in power, so that they will then be in a better position to persecute and kill the opposition, only adds to the popularity and power of the Communists.

If the United States really wants to check communism, then it must beat the Communists at their own game and provide some attractive alternatives for the groups to whom communism makes its appeal. In my country the Communist Party is powerless and discredited mostly because those who made and carried forward the Mexican Revolution were free of Marxist dogma and were able to do anything required of them better than the Marxists could. The best antidote to communism is nationalism built on a wide, popular base, and anchored on a sweeping land reform. In Bolivia, at the beginning of the 1952 revolution, the Communist Party made the grave error of opposing land reform and thereby lost all its influence. I spent some time trying to find out why they had been so stupid. They told me that a land reform backed by the United Nations (in their mythology the UN is a puppet of the United States government) was a measure designed to strengthen Yankee imperialism. Apparently, they could not have cared less about the emancipation of the Bolivian Indians. What they probably wanted was to further chaos. More recently, in Cuba, the Communist Party collaborated with Batista for years and officially opposed Castro's 26th of July movement during its formative stages.

Here a word of warning to many Latin American activists and economic planners seems necessary. While in intellectual circles there is a good deal of loose revolutionary talk inspired by grossly idealized images of the Soviet and Chinese "models," which are offered as the salvation of Latin America, among professional economists — particularly those trained in American universities — there is often an unconscious but powerful drive to imitate the American "model." Both attitudes are wrong. In view of the geographical, ethnic, historical, and cultural affinities of the Latin American countries, it seems clear that the Mexican "model" should be studied in depth. The Mexican experience has more valuable lessons to offer than any other in our contemporary world, not only because of Mexico's achievements but particularly because there is no need to repeat many of the costly errors and detours which were inevitable for the country that pioneered the way. In line with this idea, during the recent visit of President Kennedy to Mexico, a joint communiqué issued by the presidents of both countries recognized that "the Mexican Revolution and the Alliance for Progress have the same fundamental aims: social justice and economic development within a framework of individual and political freedom."

Under the circumstances described, the *Alianza* will have no other choice, at the "moment of truth," than to oppose or to favor revolutionary change. If, following current misconceptions, the United States backs the quasi-feudal and militaristic governments in power, there will be a pretense of economic development and *Alianza* funds will be misallocated and wasted without changing the conditions responsible for political unrest and economic stagnation. This will lead eventually to the establishment of military dictatorships of the extreme right.

If, following the precedents set by the Good Neighbor policy in the case of the Mexican Revolution or, later, in the case of the Bolivian Revolution, the United States learns somehow to live with popular, nationalistic, and democratically oriented movements, wherever these should emerge and however amateurish or rough they may be, favorable conditions will be created for self-help, for progress, and for better use of *Alianza* funds. Finally, if Americans oppose revolution and revolution succeeds anyway, there will be a repetition of what happened in Cuba and the Organization of American States will find itself with a dwindling membership.

MARTIN BRONFENBRENNER

The Appeal of Confiscation
in Economic Development*

"What's mine is mine, and what's yours is mine too."
Apocryphal Communist Proverb

THE appeal of confiscation in financing economic development is not "pure propaganda" in the sense of economic fallacy. It must be taken seriously, not shrugged off by easy analogies to "a shot in the arm" or "the goose that laid the golden eggs." For confiscation of capital has not killed the goose that laid the golden eggs in the Soviet Union, in China, or in the other "people's democracies." It seems rather to have been an important device permitting these countries to develop and industrialize rapidly, while other countries, in which the influence of Western ethics has been stronger, are lagging behind. It is questionable whether the lagging countries can be expected permanently to eschew the device of confiscating capital under their control unless capital is made available to them from abroad in large amounts at attractive terms; it is likewise questionable whether such largesse is in the economic interest of the lending countries.

The issue we discuss is not whether confiscation can be justified by some accepted or conventional Occidental standard of morals or propriety, but merely whether it brings the pragmatic results desired, namely economic development without sacrifice to the scale of living of the mass of the population. It will be our contention that confiscation has done so, is doing so, and will continue to do so, by shifting income to developmental investment from capitalists' consumption, from transfer abroad, and from unproductive "investment," like luxury housing. Therein lies the appeal of confiscation, although it is argued persuasively on the other side in developed countries that these accomplishments require totalitarian dictatorship for their realization and that development is not worth this price.

* Reprinted from *Economic Development and Cultural Change* by Martin Bronfenbrenner, Vol. III, No. 3 (April 1955), by permission of the University of Chicago Press.

Historical demonstration of the effects of confiscation past and present requires data from developing and developed economies on both sides of the Iron Curtain, which are not yet available in reliable form, and which may never become available at all. As an admittedly inferior substitute for historical data, I propose to "illustrate" the power of confiscation by hypothetical models of an underdeveloped overpopulated economy. The salient characteristics of this economy I shall seek to render fairly realistic for a large group of countries, but there will be others for which the model will remain completely meaningless. (The reader with time to spare may spend some of it in creating an alternative which will fit both Greenland and India, both Puerto Rico and Outer Mongolia.) The model will be sufficiently simple to remain within the bounds of primary school arithmetic. This limitation of technique will prevent consideration of bottlenecks, cyclical oscillations, balance-of-payments problems, structural relations between economic sectors, and other important effects which have been treated formally in more elaborate applications of "process analysis" to economic development.[1]

Model I. Our hypothetical economy has a net national and personal income of 100, after depreciation and before direct taxes. Income, both before and after taxes, is divided between service income[2] and property income in the proportion of 85 to 15.[3] While tax progression may be on the statute books, it plays no significant role in modifying either the functional or the personal distribution of income.[4] (Throughout this study, the reader is invited to substitute

[1] For three such applications, see J. J. Polak, "Balance of Payments Problems of Countries Reconstructing with the Help of Foreign Loans," *Quarterly Journal of Economics,* LVII (February 1943), 208–40; reprinted in American Economic Association, *Readings in the Theory of International Trade;* H. W. Singer, "The Mechanics of Economic Development," *The Indian Economic Review* (August, 1952), reprinted in the present volume, pp. 381–99; Trygve Haavelmo, *A Study in the Theory of Economic Evolution* (Amsterdam, 1954).

[2] "Service income" includes both compensation of employees and gross profits of proprietors of unincorporated enterprises. Its recipients include, along with the proletariat and peasantry, the bulk of those bourgeois segments classified in Mainland China as "petty" or "national."

[3] This property share is too high for areas in which population is scanty and land rent low. It is probably too low for densely populated areas with rich agricultural or mining land. A few statistical estimates, given below, are the best available, but refer to countries in which the property share may be lower than it is in the bulk of the underdeveloped world.

[4] One or more of the three following reasons often explains the disappointing results of progressive taxation in underdeveloped countries: (1) the extremely

Continent and country	Percentage distribution of income			
	Employee compensation	Unincorporated enterprises	Property income	Transfer payments
Africa				
Northern Rhodesia (1949)	63.6	32.7	1.4	2.3
Southern Rhodesia (1949)	55.4	33.0	8.1	3.5
Asia				
Ceylon (1951)	74.7	13.1	5.5	6.6
Japan (1949)	46.8	49.7	1.9	1.6
North America				
Puerto Rico (1948–9)	52.7	39.1		8.2
South America				
Peru (1947)	44.4	36.0	13.1	6.5

Sources: For Ceylon, unpublished data of the Central Bank of Ceylon, made available to the writer by the courtesy of Professor Theodore Morgan; for other countries, United Nations Statistical Office, "National Income and Its Distribution in Underdeveloped Countries," *United Nations Statistical Papers*, Series E, No. 3 (New York, 1951), p. 18.

his own estimates when mine appear imaginative or fantastic.)

Of the assumed property share of 15, one-third, or 5, comprises net saving (above depreciation of capital).[5] I ignore net savings out of service income as unimportant quantitatively. Of the total net savings of 5, 40 per cent (or 2) takes forms available for domestic economic development, either as capital goods or as "social overhead capital." The remainder (or 3) is dissipated in foreign investments, inventories, or residential housing of a luxury or semi-luxury variety.[6]

limited number of technically competent administration and enforcement officials; (2) the susceptibility of underpaid and overworked civil servants to direct or indirect corruption; and (3) class systems which render it improper for the mere tax-office clerk to question the returns or statements of wealthy merchants or landowners who are his social superiors.

[5] Gross saving (and investment) percentages would of course be much larger. An estimate by the United Nations Economic Commission for Latin America, for example, concludes that 14 per cent of the total income of this area entered into gross savings in 1953, but that this savings coefficient was "barely sufficient for an annual *per capita* growth of 0.9 per cent." *International Co-operation in a Latin American Development Policy* (New York, 1954).

[6] Dissipation in hoards, or in bidding up the values of land and other existing

Population is growing at the rate of 1.5 per cent a year. This last figure is compounded of a 15 per cent return on developmental investment (including a substantial write-up for external economies), a 60 per cent return on population growth (where any figure under 100 per cent indicates "diminishing returns"), and a flat 0.5 per cent for "entrepreneurship" or innovation, including particularly the introduction of methods already in vogue in other countries.[7]

With population growing at 1.5 per cent per year and aggregate income at 1.7 per cent, the annual growth rate of *per capita* income is only, to a first approximation, 0.2 per cent.[8] If there is no change in the income distribution, *per capita* service income also grows at this same rate (0.2 per cent per year). This is near-stagnation, which widens annually the developmental gap separating this economy from the advanced countries of the Western World.

These figures are summarized and presented as Table I. This

assets, may also exist. I do not consider it here because such dissipation can be counteracted with relative ease by deficit financing on the part of the government. Dissipation such as is listed in the text requires diversion of real goods from developmental investment to exports, inventories, or residential construction.

[7] For two independent estimates, one more sanguine than ours and one less so, consider the following running quotation from Joseph J. Spengler, "Demographic Patterns," in Harold F. Williamson and John A. Buttrick (eds.), *Economic Development: Principles and Patterns* (New York, 1954), pp. 77 f.:

"The movement of aggregate income is dominated by: (1) equipment or income-producing wealth; (2) technical and related forms of progress; and (3) the magnitude of the labour force. With factors (2) and (3) constant, a 1 per cent increase in the amount of 'capital' in use will be accompanied by an increase of 0.25 to 0.35 per cent in aggregate net income. With factors (1) and (2) constant, a 1 per cent increase in the labour force will be accompanied by an income increase of 0.65 to 0.75 per cent. On the basis of these estimates and of growth actually recorded in various national incomes, the forces included under (2) have been increasing net incomes in advanced countries something like 1 per cent yer year.

"Somewhat similar results were obtained by E. C. Olson in a study based on international comparisons. He found that a 1 per cent increase in the employed population was accompanied by only about 0.25 per cent increase in the national income; and that 1 per cent increases, respectively, in the total amounts of energy and livestock used, were accompanied by increases of about 0.5 and 0.25 per cent in the national income."

[8] The United Nations Economic Commission for Asia and the Far East (ECAFE) is more pessimistic. With population growing at 1.5 per cent per annum, ECAFE estimates 6 to 7 per cent net investment to be required for maintenance of existing *per capita* income under East Asian conditions. "Some Financial Aspects of Development Programmes in Asian Countries," *Economic Bulletin for Asia and the Far East* (Jan.–June 1952), pp. 1 f.

table has been expanded to include the results of 5, 10, and 20 years of growth compounded according to the assumptions which we have made.

TABLE I — THE STATUS QUO: ECONOMIC STAGNATION

Line No.	Units	Current	After 5 years	After 10 years	After 20 years
1. Real income	Absolute	100.0	108.8	118.4	140.1
2. Service income	”	85.0	92.5	100.6	119.1
3. Property income	”	15.0	16.3	17.8	21.0
4. Saving ratio	Per cent	5.0	5.0	5.0	5.0
5. Developmental investment ratio	”	2.0	2.0	2.0	2.0
6. Population growth rate	”	1.5	1.5	1.5	1.5
7. Aggregate income growth rate	”	1.7	1.7	1.7	1.7
8. *Per capita* income growth rate	”	0.2	0.2	0.2	0.2
9. *Per capita* income	Index No.	100.0	101.0	102.0	104.1
10. *Per capita* service income	”	85.0	85.0	86.7	88.5

Notes: (Line 7) = .15 (Line 5) + .60 (Line 6) + 0.5
(Line 8) = (Line 7) − (Line 6) (Approximation)

Model II. "Comes the Revolution." It may indeed be a social revolution, with or without substantial violence and destruction. It may be a capital levy at rates close to 100 per cent. It may be "nationalization," with compensation wiped out by rapid inflation.[9] At any rate, all capital goods which yield incomes become State property. Certain consumer durable goods which can be converted to income-yielding uses, or sold abroad for capital imports, also become State property. All income from this property goes to the State, none to the former property owners, even though they may retain the bare legal title to certain of the assets. None of the income from property is paid to the service-income classes directly; there is no immediate redistribution or "social dividend" in this model. Because of the absence of redistribution I call this model "Confiscation, Russian Style," with special reference to the period of the first four Five-Year Plans, although the figures I shall use cannot be applied realistically to actual Soviet experience.[10]

[9] "Nationalization" with approximately full compensation, on the British model, will not in itself bring about the increases in saving and investment which are postulated below.

[10] A critic has suggested that they might have been realistic for a Soviet Union which had succeeded in remaining neutral during World War II, or located in a world free from major wars.

More precisely, let us suppose that two-thirds of what had previously been property income (or 10 per cent of the total national income), is used by the State for development purposes broadly conceived, i.e., including not only capital goods but also "social overhead capital." The other third of what had previously been property income (or 5 per cent of the total national income) is dissipated by additional "non-productive" government expenditures[11] (public buildings, armaments, military and police personnel, etc.) or into symbolic compensation for the former property-owners. The five per cent leakage also includes income which would have been earned by private parties but which is not earned under public ownership, either because of damage during revolutionary upheaval or because of inefficient allocation by the public authorities. Income created by conversion of nationalized consumer durables (e.g., crops grown on former hunting preserves or golf courses) will be a deduction from the leakage, as will income acquired from foreign sale of other nationalized durables like jewelry and art objects.

An important point in this discussion of leakages is often misunderstood, both by Socialists and by their opponents. The Socialist need not deny the technical superiority of private gain to public interest in allocating land and capital to their most productive uses, although he usually feels compelled to do so, sometimes with reason. Neither need the Socialist deny, as he often does, the involuntary social service performed by the landlord, capitalist, or entrepreneur who makes the more efficient allocation. The Socialist need deny only that this service is worth 10, 15, or 25 per cent of the national income of a poor country, a far less plausible proposition. The Socialist can be compared in this respect to a shabby-genteel buyer of a shabby-genteel used car, who should deny only that the new model is worth to him its 50 per cent extra cost but who insists on assuaging his ego with verbiage about "they don't make them this good any more."

Returning to our theoretical scheme: Let the current year be one in which "normalcy" has been restored after the Revolution. The

---

[11] There is much to be said for rehabilitation of the classical economists' distinction between productive and non-productive activities, the former contributing to the maintenance or expansion of the level of economic development and the latter not. We must grant the distinction to be invalid in terms of the creation of utilities, and it is inaccurate to identify this distinction, as the classical economists did, with the distinction between the production of goods and the production of services. *Cf.* Paul Baran, "Economic Progress and Economic Surplus," *Science and Society*, VII (Fall 1953), pp. 290–300.

aggregate income growth rate under public control has fallen to 12.5 per cent of the developmental investment rate plus 55 per cent of the population growth rate plus an improvement or innovation factor of 0.4 per cent. The corresponding figures in Model I were 15, 60, and 0.5 respectively. The reductions are further allowances, over and beyond the five per cent leakage, for the presumably greater efficiency of private over social entrepreneurship. As for population, its rate of growth begins to increase, partially in anticipation of better days to come and partly in response to improvements as they are achieved. Over five years the (geometric) mean growth rate is 1.55 per cent, over 10 years 1.60 per cent, over 20 years 1.65 per cent, with an eventual asymptote at 1.75 per cent.[12] Nevertheless, comparing Model II with Model I, we see immediately a higher growth rate of *per capita* income, which is caused by diversion of the bulk of property income to development purposes.[13] *Per capita* service income keeps pace, despite the absence of direct redistribution, and rises at once above the near-stagnation of the status quo. Diversion of property income to developmental investment has triumphed over both the Malthusian bogey of overpopulation and the Brozenian bogey of "Fabian" entrepreneurship.[14] The triumph is only on paper and is

[12] A growth rate of 1.50 per cent in the current year, rising by 0.02 per cent per year until 1.60 per cent is reached in year 5, then by 0.01 per cent per year until 1.75 per cent is reached in year 25, will yield geometric means close to those in the text.

[13] A query from a cynical critic at this point remains unanswered: Can any government but a totalitarian dictatorship devote 10 per cent of its national income to developmental investment year after year without being voted out of office by the partisans of Santa Claus here and now? An American survey of actual Soviet experience underlines the criticism. "It may be inferred . . . that Soviet industrial growth was as rapid as it was *because of,* rather than *despite,* the existence of central planning and authoritarian control. It seems doubtful that the amount and pattern of Soviet investment would ever be duplicated in an essentially consumer-oriented market economy. . . . Such a level and pattern of investment, and the rapid economic growth which results, could only be accomplished by an economic system designed to fulfill the wishes of central planners. Resources must be directed, despite the needs and desires of households, predominantly into machines which produce machines (and weapons) rather than into machines which produce consumers' goods and services, including housing," Franklyn D. Holzman, "Soviet Economic Growth," *World Politics,* VII, No. 1 (October 1954), p. 144.

[14] Yale Brozen has become the most articulate professional spokesman in America for those economists and business leaders who consider private entrepreneurship an indispensable ingredient in economic development over the long period. His position is summarized in his essay, "Entrepreneurship and Technological Change," in Williamson and Buttrick, *op. cit.,* pp. 196–236, and this

derived from arbitrary figures, but in selecting these figures I have attempted "leaning to one side" against the appeal of confiscation, and can imagine no realistic assumptions leading to contrary qualitative conclusions in societies whose income distributions include high property shares which are not ploughed back into economic development. Table II, summarizing these results, is presented immediately below.

TABLE II — CONFISCATION, RUSSIAN STYLE

Line No.	Units	Current	After 5 years	After 10 years	After 20 years
1. Real income	Absolute	100.0	113.1	128.4	166.1
2. Service income	"	85.0	96.2	109.1	141.2
3. Property income	"	0.0	0.0	0.0	0.0
4. Saving ratio	Per cent	10.0	10.0	10.0	10.0
5. Development investment ratio	"	10.0	10.0	10.0	10.0
6. Population growth rate	"	1.50	1.55	1.60	1.65
7. Aggregate income growth rate	"	2.48	2.50	2.53	2.57
8. Per capita income growth rate	"	0.98	0.95	0.93	0.92
9. Per capita income	Index No.	100.0	104.9	119.7	120.1
10. Per capita service income	"	85.0	89.1	93.3	102.1

Notes: (Line 7) = .125 (Line 5) + .55 (Line 6) + 0.40
(Line 8) = (Line 7) — (Line 6) (Approximation)
(Line 6) and (Line 7) are geometric means over the respective time periods.

Model III. A lower rate of growth after the "Revolution," but higher personal incomes during the earlier years of development, can be obtained by diverting part of what was formerly property income for consumption purposes. In the third model, one-third of property income (5 per cent of national income, 6 per cent of service income) is redistributed to the recipients of service income, as for example by increases in industrial real wages or by replacement of high agricultural land rents by lower agricultural land taxes. Property income, in this third model, has therefore been divided into three equal parts: developmental investments, leakages, and transfers to service income.

in turn is summarized in a one-sentence quotation from W. T. Easterbrook (*ibid.*, p. 224): "The straightest, perhaps the only, road to social security is via entrepreneurial security."

An interesting and suggestive classification of entrepreneurship into "innovating," "imitative," "Fabian," and "drone" varieties, due to Clarence Danhof, is used by Brozen, *ibid.*, p. 205.

This disposal of the proceeds of confiscation to include transfers to service income I call "Chinese style," although the figures bear no intentional quantitative similarity to actual developments in Mainland China.[15]

The other assumptions of Model II are retained here, with the results presented as Table III. All the unfavourable features of Model II are retained; the leakages, the inefficiencies in resource allocation, the slowing of innovation, the increased population growth rate. Another "unfavourable" feature has been added, from the developmental point of view: redistribution of income from savers to spenders. Nevertheless, growth is more rapid than under Model I, as measured either by aggregate or *per capita* income. Growth is slower than under the "Russian-style" confiscation of Model II, but it reaches the common people more rapidly, due to the redistribution feature. (Comparing Tables I and III, no great divergence can be seen in

TABLE III — CONFISCATION, CHINESE STYLE

Line No.	Units	Current	After 5 years	After 10 years	After 20 years
1. Real income	Absolute	100.0	109.8	120.8	146.6
2. Service income	"	90.0	98.8	108.7	131.9
3. Property income	"	0.0	0.0	0.0	0.0
4. Saving ratio	Per cent	5.0	5.0	5.0	5.0
5. Developmental investment ratio	"	5.0	5.0	5.0	5.0
6. Population growth rate	"	1.50	1.55	1.60	1.65
7. Aggregate income growth	"	1.86	1.88	1.91	1.93
8. *Per capita* income growth rate	"	0.36	0.33	0.31	0.28
9. *Per capita* income	Index No.	100.0	101.7	103.4	105.8
10. *Per capita* service income	"	90.0	91.5	93.1	95.2

Notes: (Line 7) = .125 (Line 5) + .55 (Line 6) + 0.40
(Line 8) = (Line 7) — (Line 6) (Approximation)
(Line 6) and (Line 7) are geometric means over the respective time periods.

the course of income *per capita*. The divergence in service income *per capita*, the more significant item for the masses, is attributable almost entirely to redistribution on the basis of these arbitrary figures.)

Choice as between Models II and III depends upon the preferences of revolutionary societies, and still more of revolutionary leaders. Time preferences are important, and likewise the choice between

[15] It is conceivable that Russian practice after Stalin's death may be shifting closer to this model than to Model II.

high growth rates and income redistribution. As this is written (1954–5), Model III seems to exercise the greater fascination for the underdeveloped world.

Neither of the confiscation models, it should be noted, forces the common people to finance development themselves in terms of lower real incomes at any time, although the attainment of higher real incomes may be postponed in the interests of capital accumulation. Comparing either model with the status quo, it is difficult to see how any could prefer the latter, unless he be an adherent of morality *ruat coelum* or of Professor Ayres' "Divine Right of Capital." The popular appeal of confiscation appears to require less economic explanation than does the democratic resistance thereto.

Confiscation of capitalist property and property income is credited with no significant part in the economic development of Western Europe, North America, Australasia, or Japan. If our models possess any verisimilitude, this seems strange at first glance. Yet there are a number of reasons which combined to make the developing Western world safe for the capitalist in the nineteenth century, which cannot be relied upon to make the developing remainder of the world equally safe for his biological or spiritual progeny in the twentieth century. Some of these considerations relate directly to certain of the figures of our models; others involve social issues which we have been unable to reduce to numerical form. I list eight factors; no historical instance rested significantly on all eight, and no one of the eight applied significantly to all the economies which developed early.[16]

1. Highly important, except in the Japanese case, was the high social mobility which prevailed in the developing countries. In most cases, the period of rapid development seems to have been an age of "three generations from shirt-sleeves to shirt-sleeves." More significantly, it was an age in which entrepreneurship in developmental activity was a promising route from the bottom to the top of the social ladder. A large part of the population saw its future, or its descendants' future, in entrepreneurship and thereafter in property-ownership, however extravagant these visions became in the event. As a result, neither egalitarianism nor confiscation could hold great popular appeal over long periods. Social mobility in an upward direction is exceptional in the underdeveloped communities of today, and

---

[16] The development of this section was assisted significantly by Benjamin Higgins' paper on "Economic Development of Underdeveloped Areas, Past and Present," (*Land Economics,* August 1955) and by the criticisms by several friends of an earlier draft of the present essay.

such mobility as exists appears to exercise little influence on the political and economic attitudes of the people.

2. Expropriation, moreover, has seldom had in the advanced capitalist countries the aid of xenophobia which it has in much of the present-day underdeveloped world. Most of the capital in the Western countries was held by native citizens, if we except specie hoards in Italian, Jewish, or Levantine hands. These native citizens were not, like the *compradores* of China, the agents of foreign interests. When capital was foreign-held, the owners tended to be similar to native citizens in race, religion, and general mores. Ownership of capital was not associated with overbearing foreigners prejudiced against "the natives" on racial or religious grounds. Such prejudice and overbearingness as existed was primarily in the opposite direction most of the time, as witness the history of European Jewry. The contrast with present-day Asia, Africa, or Latin America need not be dwelt on further.

3. In the eighteenth and nineteenth centuries there was little of the self-conscious haste that infuses the two-to-ten-year plans of today. (Japan under the Meiji Emperor was a partial exception, as was Germany under Bismarck.) There was implicit confidence that development would come in time, by Adam Smith's "invisible hand," and relative unconcern about the precise date. The United States, for example, waited for 100 years after independence as a satisfied raw material producer, before challenging British primacy in manufacturing on the world market. During the same period, American enterprisers extended railroads ahead of their traffic and built factories beyond the market capacity for their outputs, relying on the next decade or generation (plus tariffs or subsidies, but not central planning) to justify their rashness. The underdeveloped countries of today, precisely because they have been left behind for a century or more, want to catch up in a hurry, and have no faith in market forces or private enterprise to achieve in 1950 what they did not achieve in 1850 or 1900.

4. In our Model I, only 13 per cent of property income is reinvested in domestic economic development. The appeal of confiscation would be less if this figure were higher. The figure given is probably too high for much of the present underdeveloped world. But it would have been too low for New England, Yorkshire, or the Ruhr Valley, during their periods of expansion. For these regions rose to economic greatness when the Calvinistic heritage dominated their religious scene, although Calvin himself had long passed away. The Calvinist heritage meant, in the nineteenth century as well as

the sixteenth and seventeenth, that high incomes were justified, if at all, by high saving and investment, and that luxurious consumption was frowned upon as abuse of divine stewardship. Delhi and Versailles might have exercised the same "demonstration effect" upon developing Boston and Manchester — lowering investment and disturbing the balance of payments — which Paris and Hollywood exercise on developing Latin America today. But they did not, and private capital justified itself by its works. In the present underdeveloped world, however, the drive of wealthy businessmen "to accumulate capital and expand their enterprises is continuously counteracted by the urgent desire (or social compulsion) to imitate in their living habits the socially dominant 'old families,' to prove by their conspicuous outlays that they are socially (and therefore also politically) not inferior to their aristocratic partners in the socially ruling coalition."[17] Or, as the matter is summed up by Spengler, production dominated consumption in the developing West of the eighteenth and nineteenth centuries, while consumption is tending to dominate production in the underdeveloped countries of the twentieth century.[18]

5. Conversely, eighteenth- and nineteenth-century governments were less adequately equipped to execute economic development projects than the Iron and Bamboo Curtain governments of the twentieth century. To hand over property or property income to the typical Stuart, Bourbon, or Romanoff monarch or minister would have wasted the returns and the principal as well. More chaos than progress would have resulted from State Socialism under Charles II, Louis XV, or Nicholas II. Leakages would have absorbed 100 per cent of the property income. Aesop's fable of the goose and the golden eggs would have applied. The classical economists were platitudinously right in listing the security of private property as a requisite for economic progress.[19] But as John Stuart Mill himself seems to have foreseen, this doctrine can no longer be applied without modification.[20] Although many a government of a modern underdeveloped

---

[17] Paul A. Baran, "National Economic Planning," in B. F. Haley (ed.), *Survey of Contemporary Economics,* Vol. II (Homewood, Illinois, 1952), p. 378.

[18] Joseph J. Spengler, *op. cit.,* p. 96.

[19] See, e.g., John Stuart Mill, *Principles of Political Economy* (ed. W. J. Ashley) (London, 1909), pp. 881 f.

[20] *Ibid.,* pp. 204–11, including a famous passage (p. 208):

"If, therefore, the choice were to be made between Communism with all its chances, and the present state of society with all its sufferings and injustices; if the institution of private property necessarily carried with it as a consequence,

country follows the ineffective Stuart-Bourbon-Romanoff pattern, there is usually a good chance that its revolutionary successor will not. In weighing the feasibility of a Socialist alternative to a stagnant capitalism, the present character of the existing non-Socialist government (viz. the Kuomintang of Chiang Kai-shek) should often be given less weight than the anticipated character of its Socialist rival (in this case, the Chinese Communist Party).

6. Confiscation of capitalist property and its income may have played no great part in the economic development of the Western world, but other forms of confiscation were not avoided. The natural resources of America, Canada, Australia, New Zealand, South Africa were confiscated from aboriginal tribes. Individual and communal rights of the English peasantry were confiscated piecemeal over the three or four centuries of the enclosure movement. Feudal baronies in France and ecclesiastical properties in England, rice subventions of Japanese *samurai*, were all confiscated by the State and converted largely to private developmental uses as incidents of the French Revolution, the English Reformation, and the Westernization of Japan. So great was the loot of Bengal that Premier Nehru can speak, with no more than pardonable patriotic exaggeration, of the British industrial revolution of the eighteenth century being financed through the proceeds of confiscated Indian capital.[22] One is reminded of Karl Marx on "The Genesis of the Industrial Capitalist": "If money . . . comes into the world with a congenital blood-stain on one cheek, capital comes dripping from head to foot, from every pore, with blood and dirt."[23]

7. With such exceptions as have been mentioned, the legitimacy of private property rights, acquired through purchase or bequest, has been recognized throughout the Western world throughout the period of Western economic development. It has become too fundamental a part of the Western legal system to succumb to immediate frontal assault. But under the impact of international collectivist ideologies,

that the produce of labour should be apportioned as we now see it, almost in an inverse ratio to the labour . . . if this or Communism were the alternative, all the difficulties, great or small, of Communism would be but as dust in the balance."

21 Although Americans, for example, should not forget the wholesale debt repudiations of the Midwestern and South Central States following the Panic of 1837.

22 Jawaharlal Nehru, *The Discovery of India* (New York: John Day, 1946), p. 296 f., citing also Brooks Adams, *The Law of Civilization and Decay.*

23 Karl Marx, *Capital*, Vol. I (Chicago, 1906), p. 834.

the "legitimacy" concept of property rights is following the "legitimacy" concept of royal sovereignty into the discard in country after
country, where it has become less firmly and honourably established.
This is particularly true when, as in such cases as the *zamindari* of
India, or the oil concessions of Iran, "legitimate" ownership rights are
traceable to questionable transactions in a relatively recent past.

8. Some developed countries (Japan being perhaps the best example) accumulated the bulk of the capital for their development
from the masses of the people. In Japan this was done by keeping
the peasants at the subsistence level through increasing land taxes
(which were shifted generally to the tenant farmers),[24] and holding
real wages down through inflation and monopsonistic labour market
practices. But the peasants and workers of most underdeveloped
countries have become too well enlightened by Leftist leaders, and
have come to possess too much military and political strength, for such
alternatives to confiscation to be widely effective in raising capital
in the latter half of the twentieth century.[25]

Confiscation of property and property income runs counter to
Western notions of economic morality. More important, it runs
counter to Western economic interests. For when property is expropriated, foreign property will usually be expropriated earlier and on
less considerate terms than domestic.[26] Western nations are therefore
doubly concerned with the appeal of confiscation in underdeveloped
countries. If, as I believe, the appeal of confiscation makes economic
sense, it will probably increase with time. The question arises: How
should Western policy meet the ideological and the practical threats
to Western interests?

[24] Shifting of land taxes to tenants implies a situation in which landlords
were not exacting maximum rentals from tenants before the taxes were imposed
or increased. The feudal landlords in Japan prior to the Meiji Restoration were
far from economic men, and probably failed in many cases to collect the full
rental value of their properties.

[25] The principal exception to this generalization is found where the Government forces crop deliveries at low fixed prices, and then resells them at higher
market prices, the profit going largely for development purposes. (Thailand
and Burma, for example, gain large revenues from this system of rice market-
ing.) If the analysis in the text is correct, such regressive taxation of the
peasantry will not continue politically feasible for many years after the peasants
are informed (as they are being informed) of the economic significance of the
two-price policies.

[26] There are many exceptions to this general statement (e.g., Yugoslavia
under Marshal Tito), usually involving political relations between the expropriating country and the homelands of the foreign investors.

The optimum solution, from the Western point of view, would be a reformist, voluntary "democratic alternative," which would provide growth rates comparable to those of our Models II and III without the concomitant expropriation of foreign and domestic property.[27] Many such "democratic alternatives" may be found on paper: taxation (other than capital levies), increased saving by propertied classes, "mobilizing" this saving for development purposes, and so on. Efforts in these directions are laudable, and nothing said here should be interpreted in their disparagement. However, I shall make the pessimistic assumption in the remainder of this paper that, for much of the underdeveloped world, any "democratic" or "voluntary" alternative is too little and comes too late — that it is, in other words, Utopian — so that the appeal of confiscation must be answered by suppression of revolutionary movements and/or through sweetening of the *status quo* through economic aid from Western sources.

The traditional way of dealing with backward peoples' disregard of advanced Western concepts of property rights has been suppression, and the traditional mechanism of suppression has been a species of the genus "imperialism." The precepts of Western business etiquette and the interests of Western economic adventurers were enforced simultaneously upon the "lesser breeds without the Law." Offending countries became colonies, dependencies, protectorates, satellites, "spheres of influence," or were otherwise disciplined. This was "gunboat diplomacy." But the gunboat diplomacy species of imperialism has passed with its prophet, Rudyard Kipling. There will doubtless remain for some time areas in which one or another Power finds an aerial version of gunboat diplomacy effective in enforcing the economic proprieties in the interests of its influential citizens. (Kenya in Africa and Gautemala in Central America come to mind, in the context of the middle 1950s.) But such areas are apparently shrinking rather than expanding, and gunboat diplomacy has come not always to pay even where it still works. That is to say, the enmities which it creates are becoming more widespread and therefore more costly to combat around the globe and in the long run than is justified by the value of the capital it preserves in the limited area still open to its use. A country forcibly restrained from expropriating

[27] Critics have suggested another optimum solution, from the Western point of view: the indefinite renunciation of economic development by the "backward" two-thirds of the world's population. This is (almost) certainly wrong. Almost any development short of autarchy creates customers and suppliers for the rest of the world faster than it creates competitors — special cases to the contrary notwithstanding.

property income this year may go "behind the Curtain" in the next. Or its example will be used to move some other country Leftward (or Eastward, as the case may be).

Imperialistic repression of confiscation now operates generally in disguise, as a necessary concession to world-wide nationalistic aspirations. Its usual present form is the supply of military assistance to maintain in power governments in underdeveloped countries which can be trusted not to confiscate foreign property, however little may be said for them on other grounds and however little support they may be able to generate among their subjects. But many of the objections to gunboat diplomacy apparently apply with almost equal force to this successor. It too often fails, outside the military orbit of some Western power. And when it succeeds, it too may not be worth its cost in the long run, when the regime maintained in power is a stench in its neighbours' nostrils and the method of maintenance alienates these neighbours politically and economically.

The expectation of rewards for good behaviour, in the form of future foreign loans and investments, seems already much more efficacious in forestalling expropriation than is the fear of punishment or the bolstering of "friendly" governments by military aid. When a country stands to lose more in future aid by confiscating private capital within its control than it stands to gain from the value of the capital at stake, it usually exercises a seemly caution and restraint in dealing with private interests affiliated with sources of potential largesse. But the hope or the promise of reward must be substantial, plausible, and contemporary. Crumbs from the table will not do, nor pie in the sky when you die. Here lies the rub, for those benevolent global planners in the United States and the international agencies who hope to forestall confiscatory financing indefinitely by a spate of kind words and a few billion dollars spread thinly in time and space over the underdeveloped world.

Once the loans and investments are made, moreover, their expansion cannot end easily. Capital sunk at long term in a foreign land is, like a wife and children, a hostage to fortune. (In this case, a hostage to expropriation.) The hostage may be safeguarded by additional capital, or promises thereof. When made, these additional loans and investments become ransoms to expropriation. Like other ransoms, they must be large and they must eventually be delivered. Unlike other ransoms, each payment becomes another hostage to be ransomed. As the total hostage of capital increases, the greater the temptation it presents to the confiscator, and the greater the ransom required for its continued protection. The greater becomes the value of existing foreign investment required continuously to safeguard it against expropriation.[28]

The attempt by the West to bribe or buy its way out of confiscation of its investments in the underdeveloped countries may yet become the white man's burden of the twentieth century. It is costly enough in the present, to taxpayers in the advanced countries and to victims of inflation and material shortages. What is more alarming is that each instalment paid on the cost will increase rather than decrease the cost of each subsequent instalment, with no upper bound in sight until the borrowing country has achieved development at a rate satisfactory to its leaders.

In these circumstances, my own suggestion is for withdrawal, for "economic neo-isolation" of the developed from the underdeveloped world. It is less a suggestion for a new policy, in fact, than a franker and more brutal recognition of the nature of present Western policy, and for undeceiving the underdeveloped countries regarding prospects for early relaxation.

Capital remains scarce, despite gloomy forecasts of its superfluity in "mature economies." It remains scarce for purely domestic uses both civil and military.[29] Capital being scarce, the advanced countries give first priority to their domestic needs, and distribute it for development in the rest of the world only on a cautious and niggardly scale. They make it available abroad — in quantity, that is to say — only at going rates of interest, and under acceptable guarantees against not only expropriation but also freezing of interest, profits, and principal repayments.

Neo-isolation, as I see it, is little beyond explicit recognition of the facts if I see them aright, and a resulting limitation of government (and government-guaranteed) development loans within the same quantitative limits as the charitable grants typified by the American Point Four programme, however meagre and unsatisfactory these limits may seem to developing countries. Neo-isolation, if adopted as formal policy, would mean saying (as against hinting) to the governments of the underdeveloped countries: "We appreciate and sympathize with your desire for economic progress. Therefore we recognize the appeal of expropriation in financing economic development, if not to yourselves then to your successors in office.

28 In this discussion I consider the absolute volume of new investment, not its proportion to the national income of the investing country.

29 I need not face the issue here as to whether the scarcity would survive reduction of Western defence expenditures to the level of the 1920s.

We recognize as well the economic soundness of confiscation, from your point of view. We therefore feel it unsafe to lend you appreciably more than we can afford to present you free of charge. We are unwilling to assume a financial 'white man's burden' of ransoming an increasing volume of existing loans and investments from confiscation by an increasing volume of new ones. If private individuals and international associations are more venturesome, well and good, but we are unwilling to underwrite their ventures."

Such bluntness and brutality would lead to an immediate disadvantage to the West. It would accelerate, by decades if not by generations, the evil day of expropriation of existing Western assets in many countries, although (if the previous argument is correct) it would reduce total Western losses from the expropriation process. Neo-isolation would also raise delicate questions of relations with expropriating governments, and questions of possible domestic compensation to the owners of the confiscated foreign assets. These questions involve details which must be worked out differently in each case, but certain general rules may apply and may be useful:

1. Diplomatic relations with confiscating governments should not be broken off.

2. No more favourable treatment should be demanded for Western nationals in the event of confiscation than is given to citizens of the confiscating country. (If more favourable treatment is offered, without pressure, there is no reason for non-acceptance.) Equality of treatment should ordinarily be striven for; it cannot always be achieved.

3. Domestic compensation for victims of foreign expropriation should neither be promised nor ruled out wholesale. Amounts to be paid should be estimated on the merits of individual cases, with consideration for (a) the manner in which the property was acquired, (b) the historical and reproduction cost of the assets confiscated, (c) the record of the claimant's relations with the government and people of the confiscating country prior to confiscation, and (d) the returns already paid prior to confiscation. If guarantees of domestic compensation are made to enterprisers of particular foreign projects, they should be conditional upon satisfactory performance on points (a) and (c) above, upon application of the "prudent investment" principle under point (b), and upon moderation under point (d). Compensation should not be paid for unrealized capital gains from speculation in real estate or in inventories.

Underdeveloped areas are not all alike. There are many in which our pessimistic models do not apply. There are many in which a "democratic alternative" to both stagnation and confiscation is in actual operation. There is no uniform treadmill which one may call "The Political Economy of Backwardness."[30] For this reason among others, there are many countries in which confiscation is not a near-term problem. In these countries, a defeatist neo-isolation policy should not be applied. It is not in fact being applied there; statistical analysis shows Western aid concentrated in such countries, to an extent otherwise incomprehensibly disproportionate.[31]

What are the underdeveloped areas to which neo-isolation is inappropriate? There would appear to be five major categories in which large-scale international lending for development purposes seems appropriate, and in most of which it is in fact being carried on.

1. Isolation would be mistaken, first of all, in areas which, while technically underdeveloped, have already attained high living standards and rapid social mobility upwards. Here confiscation exercises no more appeal than it did on the nineteenth-century American frontier. These are the areas *par excellence* of successful "democratic alternatives" to both stagnation and expropriation. Alaska, Labrador, and perhaps Brazil provide examples. Illustrations from Asia, from Africa, or from heavily populated regions generally are difficult if not impossible to find.

2. At the other end of the scale, isolation need not be applied in those areas in which there is nothing worth confiscating, i.e. in which there is neither property income nor luxury consumption on any scale. Libya, Afghanistan, and Nepal are examples. Loans and investments here may or may not be productive, but they will probably be safe from expropriation unless these countries are taken over by Communist aggression, unless the investments themselves create a leisure class as target for expropriation, or unless the burden of interest charges and principal repayments is set too high for the countries to meet while still developing at reasonable rates.

[30] For an opposite view, *cf.* Paul A. Baran, "On the Political Economy of Backwardness," as well as other writings already cited in this essay. Baran is more right than wrong in his neo-Marxian analyses. His writings are a welcome antidote to the Pollyanna pronunciamentos of some official agencies and the unfounded confidence in "pragmatism" (or "muddling through") of the remainder. Baran suffers nevertheless from the oversimplification of identifying every backward area with every other, with the Poland of the inter-war "Colonels' Clique" as the possible archetype.

[31] Concentration of Western loans and investments in areas where confiscation is not threatened may conceivably, if the results are favourable, exercise some degree of contagion on the remainder of the underdeveloped world, and reduce somewhat the general threat of confiscation.

3. Isolation should not apply, thirdly, where the yield of capital is high enough to satisfy simultaneously the demands of foreign investors and the aspirations of domestic political leaders. Regions rich in natural resources, particularly petroleum, fall into this category: Saudi Arabia in the Middle East, Venezuela in South America, Brunei on the island of Borneo. Paradoxically, this category also includes many of the "new democracies," where confiscation has already occurred and a rapid growth rate has already been attained. A foreign loan to the Soviet Union, which expropriated all pre-1917 foreign investments in Russia, would be a safer economic proposition than a foreign loan to, let us say, Cambodia, in which confiscation of Western assets has never been permitted. Reluctance or refusal to consider investment in loans to socialist states is ascribable more readily to resentment of the past than to timorousness for the future.

4. Isolation is also ill-advised in areas where expropriation of property is ruled out by the fundamental law of a Western Power close enough to exercise effective supervision — tinged with imperialism, if you will. Puerto Rico and Cuba are cases in point here. In other areas, such as Portugal, political control seems safely in the hands of the propertied classes and their religious allies for the next generation or two, and expropriation does not loom presently as a significant political possibility.

5. The final exception pertains to instances of particularly close racial, religious, or cultural ties between developing countries and foreign sources of capital, which assuage the conflicts of interest that might otherwise occur. It would be difficult to imagine Israel, for example, defaulting on its obligations to Western Jewish communities while it retains its independence, or New Zealand defaulting on obligations to creditors in Great Britain.

But these are after all little more than exceptions. They do not disturb seriously my general anticipation of an increasing appeal of confiscation in economic growth, until the bulk of world development is financed by State expropriation of the property share of the national income. Neither do they disturb seriously my general recommendation of continued economic isolation and withdrawal from most of the non-Socialist underdeveloped world as the "least worst" policy for Western capitalism in the face of the threat implied in the appeal of confiscation. These defeatist conclusions apply particularly in Asia, where the direct influence of the Russian and Chinese expropriations is greatest, and where counter-pressures from the West can least easily be brought to bear.

PART THREE

ALTERNATIVES TO REVOLUTION

INTRODUCTION

Once a revolution takes place, a large number of changes in a society must be carried out if economic development is to be ensured. A number of observers have therefore gone on to ask if these changes can be implemented, and some measure of development achieved, before a revolution occurs. In contrast to the first six authors in this volume, who assert that it is often the case that no significant economic change is possible until after the violent shattering of a stultifying "old regime," conservatives believe that change in the structure of society is a means of preventing the smashing of a country in civil war.

The authors of the two selections that follow develop the argument that in order to manipulate a country so that peaceful economic development can take place, it is necessary to understand not only the nature of the required technical measures, but also the political processes that are possible in a particular country. These processes, in turn, reflect the underlying attitudes or ideologies held that set the limits on the economic and political choices open to it.

Both the ideologies and techniques of economic development have been studied by Professor Albert O. Hirschman, who draws on the experience of the Colombian land reform, and goes on to discuss the ways short of revolution by which reform necessary to economic development may be contrived.

One way of achieving rapid economic development—without necessarily resorting to revolution—is to draw up plans for desired economic development and then carry them out. Western countries did plan during their period of rapid economic growth; however, these plans were often drawn up at state and local rather than national levels. The desire to increase the rate of economic development and thus "catch up with the west," the lack of a tradition of strong, largely autonomous local government, and the scarcity of personnel with the skills necessary for economic planning have combined to give centralized planning a much stronger role in the development of the underdeveloped countries than it had in the development of most of the rich countries of the world. Gunnar Myrdal discusses the need for planning and the limits on the extent to which it is possible to plan in an increasingly democratic environment.

Professor Hirschman teaches at Columbia University; his most recent books are The Strategy of Economic Development and Journeys Towards Progress. Gunnar Myrdal is head of Stockholm's Institute for International Economic Studies. Among his many books, An American Dilemma is the best known, while Challenge to Affluence is the latest.

ALBERT O. HIRSCHMAN

Revolution by Stealth!
The Case for Sequential Reforms*

THOSE who systematically doubt or deny the possibility of significant social and economic progress without *prior* fundamental, and usually violent, changes in power relationships among social classes frequently cite the history of land reforms in support of their point of view. It is easy to show that land reforms which have been enacted in the context and as a consequence of a spectacular crisis situation, such as revolution or war, outnumber those brought about as a result of a victory of the land reform party at the polls or, more naïvely, because of some international expert's advice. In Latin America in

* Selections from: Albert O. Hirschman, *Journeys Towards Progress*, Twentieth Century Fund, 1963. Reprinted by permission of the author and of the Twentieth Century Fund.

particular, the Mexican, Bolivian and Cuban land reforms all occurred in the wake of drastic political and social change. While the available evidence indicates that improvements in the health, education or living standards of the urban masses hardly require social revolution as a "pre-condition," certain agrarian structures appear to be endowed with a special rigidity and have thereby provided the "pre-condition" theorists with an attractive line of defense for their views. Yet, even here, signs have appeared in various countries that change short of prior revolution (though far from smooth and peaceful) can no longer be ruled out once a society moves away from the stage at which it can properly be regarded as being essentially split into large landowners on one side and landless peons on the other.

The extent to which this area of the class struggle lends itself to infiltration, attrition, shifting alliances with other emerging social groups and similar complex tactics on the part of all the contestants is well brought out by the history of land tenure and land reform in Colombia. . . .

Revolution by Stealth?

In mid-1962 all the instruments were ready to make a reality out of agrarian reform in a Latin American country in which the "oligarchy" retained considerable economic and political power. Adoption of the Agrarian Reform Law is harder to explain than that of Law 200 in 1936. The latter had also been considered as going against the interests of the propertied classes, but it consisted primarily . . . in the legalization of situations which were the outcome of numerous de facto aggressions on private property staged by peasants in widely scattered actions. The Agrarian Reform Law goes beyond this stage since it contemplates the breaking up of existing latifundios. How could so unnatural, so unlikely an event come about?

It is easy to list some of the basic reasons. We have encountered two principal pressures through which the authorities come to the conclusion that some modification of existing land tenure conditions is necessary:

(1) Social unrest in the countryside resulting from living conditions acutely felt as intolerable is continuously signalled by spontaneous internal migrations of landless peasants, by frequent seizures of land by squatters, and by the ease with which guerrilla bands find recruits.

(2) Economic policy-makers facing inflationary pressures and balance-of-payments deficits cannot help noticing that low agricul-

tural production and productivity share in the blame for both these recurrent difficulties.

At the same time, the latifundio owners, though still influential, see their once dominant position in the social power structure weakened as the Colombian society becomes more stratified. Industrialists and even the progressive farm owners and operators cannot always be counted on to stand up in public for their backward, semi-feudal brethren, as became clear during the discussion of the territorial tax proposal of 1959.

Turning now to the more immediate circumstances leading to the Agrarian Reform Law, we must list for 1959–60 the powerful "demonstration effect" of the Cuban revolution and land reform and for 1960–61 the fact that agrarian reform suddenly became "respectable" and perhaps even financially rewarding as the Act of Bogotá first and then the Alliance for Progress proclaimed by the U. S. government gave it their support.

Furthermore, attempts at solving the problem in a benign, indirect or evolutionary fashion had long been tried and found wanting. The twin failures of, or disappointments over, colonization and taxation schemes in the fifties had prepared the intellectual climate for the acceptance of direct land distribution as the only effective measure.

From the political point of view, land reform does not suffer from the above-noted disability of land taxation. By espousing land reform a politician makes powerful enemies, to be sure, but he also makes numerous friends. Moreover, paradoxical as it may seem, land reform may be more acceptable than land taxation to the landowners themselves. In the first place, with land reform it is easier than with land taxation to provide for a basic exemption. . . through which a relatively small group of landowners is singled out as the target. In this fashion, the small and medium-size farmers, who are politically quite influential in some Colombian departments, are neutralized. In the case of land taxation a basic exemption is of course also possible, but it is likely to be smaller, especially for better lands. . . and the exemption is moreover subject to erosion through inflation. Furthermore, a tax becomes a certainty as soon as voted by the Congress whereas the expropriations envisioned by the agrarian reform law are only set in motion when the Land Reform Institute gets organized and actually makes use of the faculties given to it by the Law. The threat is therefore less immediate and, who knows, it may never become a reality for any one *individual* landowner who in his own mind attempts to decide which of the two, stiffer taxation or expropriation, is the greater evil. This may well appear to him as a choice between taxation for himself and expropriation for his neighbor and he is quite likely to favor the second alternative.

More generally, passage of the Land Reform may have been facilitated by the long tradition of issuing well-meaning and socially advanced laws and decrees which turn out to be ineffective because of lack of enforcement or clever obstruction. This tradition means that politicians, confident that nothing of importance is going to change, will frequently ostensibly favor and vote in favor of "progressive" measures because of the political advantages connected with such a stand. Yet, every once in a while, these politicians outsmart themselves by acting in this way and they find out too late that they have started up a machine which they cannot control. The chances of this occurring increase as a country begins to dispose of an assertive, talented, reform-minded middle class on which the government is likely to draw to administer its laws. Perhaps this is just what is happening in connection with Colombia's Agrarian Reform if the first steps of INCORA[1] are an earnest of future performance.

One remarkable characteristic of the process through which the Agrarian Reform Law was adopted and is being implemented still requires comment: The social group which stood to benefit most from the law—Colombia's small tenant farmers, sharecroppers, minifundio holders and landless laborers—took only a small and indirect part in its adoption. Land invasions continued to occur at scattered points of the national territory in 1960, but they cannot be compared in strength and impact to those which in the thirties led to Law 200;[2] and during the whole period of fifteen months during which the project was discussed in and out of Congress, the future beneficiaries of the bill under discussion hardly made their voices heard.

One pressure was felt strongly, however, by the leadership of the Liberal party: that of Alfonso López Michelsen's Revolutionary Liberal Movement. The MRL success in the 1960 elections meant that, to retain its following, the Liberal Party would have to prove to the electorate that the National Front government stood for more

[1] INCORA is the Colombian Institute of Agrarian Reform and is charged with the administration and implementation of the agrarian reform law. Ed.

[2] According to information supplied to the writer by the (Catholic) Federation of agricultural workers (Federación Agraria Nacional — FANAL), a constant trickle of land invasions between 1958 and 1962 affected properties covering an area of 90,000 hectares, largely in the northern departments of Magdalena, Atlántico and Bolívar which had remained quiet in the earlier phases of land conflicts. The Federation has of course precise knowledge only of those actions in which it took part itself.

than the defense of the status quo. This was the more important as in 1962 the Liberals would be called upon — according to the National Front formula — to vote for a Conservative President, a most bitter pill to swallow for Colombia's Liberals and one which stood in great need of some sweetening. In becoming the champion of the Reform, Carlos Lleras was thus responding to basic political realities and pressures of mass opinion. Nevertheless, he conducted his campaign for the adoption of the Reform largely on the level of parliamentary party politics, without appeal to active mass or pressure-group support or action even though he did make a number of speeches in favor of the Reform in the provinces and to audiences that included presumably some campesinos.

Carlos Lleras probably felt that he had enough trump cards in his game and he may even have judged that a direct appeal to the "masses" for support might do more harm than good by frightening those in both parties who would vote for the law in the hopeful belief that it would largely remain on paper. As undisputed leader of the Liberals it was rather easy for him to bring the recalcitrant members of his own party — and there were many — in line behind the project. At the same time, he could exert considerable pressure on the Ospina Conservatives who shared in the government and who needed Lleras' support to have their presidential nominee endorsed as the common candidate of both National Front parties.

"Revolution by stealth" — this is almost how one is tempted to describe, with a mixture of admiration and disbelief, the process by which the possibility of effecting basic changes in the country's agricultural structure has been introduced. In the course of the first seven months of 1962, as the regulatory decrees were issued, a society dominated by traditional power groups noticed with shocked surprise that it had introduced into its own midst a Trojan Horse, an infernal machine called INCORA which seemed to take seriously its mission to "reform the social agrarian structure by means of procedures designed to eliminate and prevent the inequitable concentration of landed property or its anti-economic dispersion."[3] A new fight was now in the making and its outcome would depend in large measure on the attitude of Colombia's newly elected President, Guillermo León Valencia. But it became increasingly likely that INCORA, operating in the open and already subjected to increasingly ferocious attacks from those whose interests it threatened, would now need that direct support from public opinion which had not been invoked

[3] Quoted from Art. 1 of Law 135.

earlier. The parallel with Brazil's SUDENE,[4] which had suddenly felt the need for mass support when its continued existence and authority was threatened in 1961, is suggestive here. And, in any event, is it not a pity for a country to exclude the public from viewing, applauding and *living* what is surely one of its finest hours?. . .

The Contriving of Reform

At one point. . . , the problem-solving process was described in terms of concurrent or sequential advances in understanding and motivation. For an important group of problem-solving situations these two elements are overshadowed by, and indissolubly linked with, a third condition for advance: the ability to enact and carry through certain measures, remedies, or *reforms,* in spite of the resistance which they evoke. We now turn to such situations; they are of special interest in Latin America today and occupy a prominent place in each one of our country studies.

The Reformer's Initial Handicap

Faced with the claims of the Cuban revolution on the one hand, and with the demands and promises of the Alliance for Progress on the other, Latin Americans appear to have been placed squarely before the familiar, if stark, alternative: change through violent revolution or through peaceful reform?

On the basis of the country studies it will be argued in the following pages that this traditional dichotomy does very poorly at catching the reality of social and economic change. But first it should perhaps be explained that, contrary to what might be expected, a strong initial advantage for the advocates of revolution results from formulating the choice facing the developing countries of Latin America in this bipolar fashion.

Social reform and social revolution are usually distinguished by the manner in which a given change is brought about as well as by the extent of that change. But they have in common the nature of the change, since both propose a shift in power and wealth from one group to another. Hence they are varieties of what we shall call *antagonistic* solutions to problems in contrast to *nonantagonistic* solutions which consist of measures that are expected to leave each group better or at least as well off as before.

A proposed change can be thought of as non-antagonistic by its

[4] The Northeast Development Agency. Ed.

advocates, but may turn out to be antagonistic and to be perceived as such. In fact, any "progress," however non-antagonistic it was meant to be, will almost always hurt the absolute or relative position of *some* social group, at least initially. Anthropologists have shown that all aspects of the status quo, even those that seem wholly undesirable, have their defenders and profiteers who are going to fight the proffered improvements. Unrealistic expectation of universal cooperation with measures which in the mind of their sponsors had no antagonistic component has spelled the failure of many a technical assistance project. Such disappointments have been well documented even in the ostensibly most non-antagonistic field of public health.[5] Thus we tend consistently to *underestimate* the difficulties of change in the case of (subjectively) non-antagonistic measures and we are constantly surprised and chagrined by the resistances which they encounter.

The opposite bias — overestimate of the difficulties of change — frequently affects measures which are openly and avowedly antagonistic. We know and expect that land expropriation, nationalization of industries or progressive income taxation will be strongly opposed by well-entrenched groups.[6] Hence, when it comes to such measures, the revolutionary who is out to ridicule the peaceful reformer has an easy task indeed. He will show that a basic transformation of existing power relationships is a prerequisite to adopting and enforcing any measure that threatens the interests and privileges of the ruling class. He will deride the argument that the establishment of democratic institutions and of universal suffrage will allow basic reforms to be adopted legally since, so he will argue, democratic trappings will be discarded as soon as the real powerholders find them no longer convenient.

This argument was first deployed at the beginning of the century by orthodox Marxists who disputed the emerging belief of the so-called Revisionists among the German Social-Democrats that the

[5] Oscar Lewis, "Medicine and Politics in a Mexican Village," in Benjamin D. Paul, ed., *Health, Culture and Community*, Russell Sage Foundation, New York, 1955.

[6] It is usual, but no longer justified, to limit discussion of such measures to those that are antagonistic to the interests of the older and wealthier ruling groups. More and more frequently, some Latin American countries such as Argentina and Brazil have found it imperative to tackle pressing problems of efficiency and financial solvency by curtailing the privileges of certain strategically located groups among the middle or working classes. What experience we have with this variety of antagonistic measures shows that they are no less difficult to push through than those directed against the older ruling groups.

conditions of the working class could be improved through the trade union movement and exploitative capitalism evolve peacefully into a more acceptable economic system. Pitted against Eduard Bernstein, the founder of Revisionism, Karl Kautsky, then the guardian of Marxist purity in the Social Democratic Party, exclaimed: "Does anyone believe that this victory [of the proletariat] is possible without catastrophe? I desire it, but I don't believe it."[7]

This point of view was eloquently and unremittingly reaffirmed by Harold Laski in the thirties when he predicted that even though the Labor Party might come to power legally, it would be unable to carry out its program of nationalizations:

> The central weakness [of the orthodox Labor position] is due to the refusal of the Labor Party to recognize that the state is the instrument of that class in society which owns the instruments of production and that it cannot utilize that state for its own purposes so long as that class remains in possession of those instruments. . . . Unless a Labor government is prepared to meet a crisis of the first magnitude the forces it will encounter will persuade it rather to operate the capitalist system than to move to its transformation.[8]

More recently the argument, a bit battered from successful experience with reform in the industrial countries of the West, has migrated to the less developed areas. Here, it retains greater plausibility, and, on occasion, considerable validity, for these areas frequently lack a solid tradition of progressive political and economic change. John Kenneth Galbraith was perhaps the first to refurbish the argument for its new use:

> Unfortunately, some of our current discussion of land reform in the underdeveloped countries proceeds as though this reform were something that a government proclaims on any fine morning — that it gives land to the tenants as it might give pensions to old soldiers or as it might reform the administration of justice. In fact, a land reform is a revolutionary step; it passes power, property, and status from one group in the community to another. If the government of the country is dominated or strongly influenced by the land-holding groups — the one that is losing its prerogatives — no one should expect effective land legislation as an act of grace.[9]

[7] Quoted in Peter Gay, *The Dilemma of Democratic Socialism,* Columbia University Press, New York, 1952, p. 65.

[8] Harold J. Laski, *Parliamentary Government in England,* Viking, New York, 1938, pp. 159–161.

[9] J. K. Galbraith, "Conditions for Economic Change in Under-Developed Countries," *Journal of Farm Economics,* November 1951, p. 695.

At almost the same time the argument, as applied to under-developed countries, was put back into traditional Marxist terms by Paul Baran:

The alliance of property-owning classes controlling the destinies of most underdeveloped countries, cannot be expected to design and to execute a set of measures running counter to each and all of their immediate vested interests. If to appease the restive public, blueprints of progressive measures such as agrarian reform, equitable tax legislation, etc., are officially announced, their enforcement is wilfully sabotaged. The government, representing a political compromise between landed and business interests, cannot suppress the wasteful management of landed estates and the conspicuous consumption on the part of the aristocracy; . . . Set up to guard and to abet the existing property rights and privileges, it cannot become the architect of a policy calculated to destroy the privileges standing in the way of economic progress and to place the property and the incomes derived from it at the service of society as a whole.[10]

This point of view is readily accepted in Latin America where a non-Marxist Chilean writer and politician put the same thought quite succinctly some fifty years ago.

Nobody would believe in a law which would injure the interests of the privileged class. It would be the same as if in Russia a law were passed which ordered the Czar to be shot: nobody would believe in the law.[11]

Compared to these reminders of what is and is not credible and feasible when power is distributed in a certain way, the routine of present-day international experts in blandly proposing year-in, year-out essentially antagonistic measures of every description regardless of political realities seems singularly inane or naïve. In fact, the experts themselves, after having absorbed a critical amount of frustration, frequently become converts to the view that, in this or that country, "everything" has to change before any improvement at all can be introduced.[12]

The idea of revolution as a prerequisite to any progress draws immense strength from the very limited human ability to visualize

---

[10] "On the Political Economy of Backwardness," *The Manchester School,* January 1952. . . .

[11] Alberto Edwards speaking in the Chilean Congress in 1909, quoted by Fetter, *Inflation,* pp. 126–127.

[12] An extreme illustration of this mood is the Rio cabdriver who, caught in that city's famous rush-hour jam, remarked to us: "What we need here is a Fidel Castro!" He was obviously convinced that traffic flow cannot be improved in Brazil without a prior social revolution.

change and from the fact that it makes only minimal demands on that ability. All we are asked to imagine by the revolutionary is the tumbling down of the old regime in a total upheaval which will give birth to the new order. Revolution thus conceived is essentially a quite brief, though cataclysmic interlude between two static societies: one, unjust and rotten, which is incapable of being improved, and the other, rational and harmonious, which has no further need to be improved upon. Sorel, the apostle of the violent general strike as an energizing myth, clearly had this concept of revolution in mind when he wrote:

. . . the general strike must be considered as an undivided whole; consequently, no detail about ways and means is of the slightest help for the understanding of socialism. It must even be added that there is always danger of losing something of this understanding, if one attempts to split this whole into parts . . . the transition from capitalism to socialism must be conceived as a catastrophe whose process defies description.[13]

Sorel thus understood perfectly the dual function of the idea of revolution: to gratify the desire for change and to dispense with the need to visualize the process of change in its intricate and perhaps unpleasant details by telescoping it into an "undivided whole."

The neat trick involved in this operation, while intellectually not very respectable, goes far toward explaining the drawing power of the idea of revolution. But the reformers are also to blame. They have made themselves particularly vulnerable to the charge of being unrealistic by failing to explore how social change short of cataclysmic revolution actually happens. Thus they have permitted the revolutionists to set up a caricature of "change via reform" where the latter follows smoothly (and unbelievably) upon the 51 per cent election victory of the Reform Party or, more modernly though even more naïvely, upon the recommendations of international experts or the offer of finance. Actually there are a good many intermediate stations between this kind of effortless and painless reform at one extreme and total revolution at the other and our studies permit us to map out a few of these stations.

Events of recent years have created a somewhat similar continuum between total peace and total war (cold, phony, brushfire, limited war), and political scientists have identified various types of political regimes (tutelary democracy, modernizing oligarchies) filling the void between Western-type parliamentary democracy and

[13] Georges Sorel, *Réflexions sur la violence*, 11th ed., Marcel Riviere, Paris, 1950, pp. 185, 217.

totalitarian autocracy.[14] In contrast to these efforts, our observations do not lead to the firm establishment of a typology. Rather, we shall attempt to show how elements of both reform and revolution are present in the sequences of policy-making which we have studied. In the process we hope to provide basic materials for what may eventually go into a "reformmonger's manual"; perhaps it is time that such a text be written and offer some competition to the many handbooks on the techniques of revolutions, coups d'état, and guerilla warfare.

This section stands in need of an important postscript. Our argument, as developed so far, does not mean to imply that any reform whatever can always be introduced without revolution, i.e., without the prior, violent, wholesale overthrow of the current power holders. Certainly many situations have existed and still exist in Latin America as elsewhere in which power is so concentrated, opposition to change so fierce, and the social and political structure so rigid that any non-revolutionary change is, short of a miracle, impossible, *besides* being inconceivable. The point we have been trying to make is that there are many other, less rigid situations in which change by methods short of revolution is or has become possible, but where, because of the force of habit or some similar cultural lag, change is still visualized primarily as something that requires a prior revolution. This contrast between reality and the widely entertained image of reality seems to the writer to prevail in much of Latin America today. A similar contrast with opposite content characterizes the present intellectual and political climate in the United States where, as a result of positive experience with gradualism, a majority appears to have come to the unwarranted conclusion that any progressive change whatever can and must be achieved exclusively by a succession of moderate reforms or cannot be achieved at all.[15] This can be just as much an illusion as the opposite belief of many Latin Americans that any "real" change can only come through revolution.

Violence as an Ingredient of Reform

Our statement that reform and revolution are not nearly as far apart

---

[14] Edward Shils, *Political Development in the New States,* Mouton & Co., The Hague, 1962.

[15] The exasperating slowness of racial desegregation in the United States has led to considerable soul-searching on this score, most forcefully expressed in the writings of James Baldwin. See also Eric F. Goldman, "Progress — By Moderation *and* Agitation," *The New York Times Magazine,* June 18, 1961.

as language would make us believe holds up well when we consider the role of violence. The received idea is that revolutions are violent and reforms peaceful. But if we applied this criterion for distinguishing between reform and revolution to the history of land tenure problems in Colombia, we would immediately have to conclude that Colombia has passed not through one but through several agrarian revolutions. Yet the historical record knows of no such revolution.

On reflection it will be realized that even if violence is a necessary condition for revolution it is not a sufficient one, and that it is also a common element of reform. To qualify as revolutionary, violence must be *centralized;* it must attack and conquer the central seats of political and administrative power. In Colombia violence has been scattered, local, decentralized. For the past hundred years, peasants have occupied and are still occupying today lands that are not theirs. Sometimes they have used force and force has occasionally been used against them by those who claim ownership. But eventually forcible appropriation of large areas has been sanctioned by the state through *ad hoc* intervention or general legislation. Thus, the willingness of the peasants to occupy uncultivated lands — a kind of entrepreneurial spirit — has powerfully contributed to reform legislation. Without the past experience of mass squatting and the threat of more to come, neither Law 200 of 1936 nor the land reform of 1961 would ever have been passed by the Congress.

In Brazil's Northeast, decentralized violence appears in a different guise. It is first unloosened by nature itself which, through its droughts, periodically chases hundreds of thousands of nordestinos from their homes in search of food, water and work. Relief shipments and the organization of emergency public works are an automatic response to the overriding need of social and physical survival so that it may well be said that, whenever a drought strikes, minimal needs of subsistence are "appropriated" by the Northeastern refugees. When the relief funds are not forthcoming with sufficient promptness, looting of food stores in the cities by the drought refugees serves as a reminder. This sudden and forcible appropriation of public monies by the Northeast leads subsequently to a whole chain of attempts to disburse the monies in such a way as to limit the damage that will be wrought by future droughts.

Since violence has in part the function of signalling protest to the central authorities, an improvement in the signalling mechanism serves to increase pressure as much as an intensification of the problem. Something of this kind happened in the Northeast when better and more numerous highways (built largely during droughts) and the availability of trucks permitted the miserable drought refugees to reach the coastal cities more rapidly and in greater numbers and thereby increased the threat to public order consequent upon the droughts.

As though the violent immediate reactions to the violence of nature were not enough, Northeasterners have been casting around for additional stimulants to action in the form of threatened violence. The traditional threat has been that of secession. Yet the threat of this particular violence always remained a bit rhetorical and ineffectual for lack of credibility. For one, it seemed an irrational move since it would cut off the Northeast from the principal source of relief and investment funds. Secondly, the threat is really one of an all-out centralized clash; it cannot be graduated since a region cannot secede "just a little bit." In both respects the Colombian squatter's kind of violence is more efficient, and its Brazilian counterpart has recently come into prominence in the Northeast through the activities of the peasant leagues. The creation of the new development agency in the Northeast (SUDENE) was originally rather a response to the 1958 drought, but the threat implicit in the rise of the peasant leagues strengthened the agency, which could now claim that its reform program represented the only alternative to a violent and disorderly change in the existing power structure in the Northeast.

In addition to being decentralized rather than centralized, the violence we have encountered in Colombia and Brazil is distinguished from revolutionary violence by the fact that it is not immediately countered by the aggrieved party. The violence one meets with is unilateral, sequential, *temporarily unrequited.* Land is "grabbed" by peasants, but ordinarily no immediate resistance follows. There may be action in the local courts and eventually forcible eviction of the squatters by the police and occasionally the army. Or again nothing may happen for a long time; and when the state believes it important that uncertainty be removed, but does not wish to use force to evict the peasants, it may buy the property from the owner and then attempt to sell it back to the peasant who already holds it, but still is ready to pay something for the much-coveted title which, among other advantages, makes it possible to obtain credit.

Thus the violence that is compatible with reform and frequently appears to be part and parcel of it is not the kind of decisive clash — force meets force in the principal square of the capital — which is usually associated with revolutionary violence. Rather it is a violence akin to guerrilla warfare, with the ability of the groups practicing it to now advance, now retreat, now lie low and now come forward with a new thrust.

As shown in the chapter on Chile, the economic behavior underlying inflation is rather similar to the temporarily unrequited violence practiced by squatting peasants and retaliating landlords. Inflation results typically when demands for additional money income on the part of one social group are not resisted immediately and fiercely, but are countered indirectly and after some time interval by similar demands on the part of other groups. In this perspective, inflation appears as a device for the coexistence of several groups who are not hostile or do not feel strong enough to engage in out-and-out revolutionary battles or civil war over the distribution of the social product, yet are not friendly enough either to agree on any one pattern of dividing up the product among themselves. There is reluctance to agree, but also reluctance to disagree to the point of revolution or civil war. This is at least one interpretation that can be given to the Chilean inflation of the last twenty years.

At the same time inflation is sufficiently unpleasant to lead to a search for its cause and cure, and since nothing is easier than to establish a causal nexus between one social evil (such as inflation) and another (such as maldistribution of land), inflation has served the function of putting additional pressure behind a variety of reforms which were suddenly found to be desirable not only on their own merits but also because they would help set an end to inflation. Just as the squatting actions of Colombian peasants put more "steam" behind agrarian reform projects and the droughts in the Northeast regularly led to new initiatives in favor of that area, so inflationary pressures have served as a kind of generalized, all-purpose "steam" behind any improvement in Chile's economic and social structure that caught the eye of the reformers.

A final characteristic of the violence we have met in our studies is that it is not only *protest* and *pressure* on problem-solving authorities, but also *direct problem-solving activity*. The Colombian peasant satisfies his craving for a piece of land when he squats and the Northeastern drought refugee solves his immediate problem of hunger when he loots food stores in the coastal cities as does the Chilean worker when he wins higher wages through strikes. Hence, these individual decentralized actions not only signal a problem to the central decision-makers, but they reduce the size of the problem that remains to be solved by the authorities. In effect, they therefore make at least this problem more manageable, hence more amenable to reform moves (while quite possibly creating new problems elsewhere). In Colombia, for example, it would have been unthinkable for any non-revolutionary government in the twenties or thirties to carry out through centralized action the splitting up of the large estates which actually took place as a result of decentralized, spontaneous peasant movements. But once these events had taken place the New Deal government of Alfonso López was able after a long fight to convince Congress to legalize the peasants' actions through Law 200 of 1936. Instead of the sequence: revolution (centralized violence) → redistribution of land under conditions of revolutionary legality, the Colombians invented a highly disorderly sequence: decentralized violence and illegal redistribution of land → legalization of redistribution through Law 200. Disorderly though it was, this sequence permitted an improvement in the distribution of land.

The Latin American scene thus appears to be replete with mechanisms and sequences which permit the exertion of powerful pressures and the venting and adjudication of conflicts by means equally far removed from traditional concepts of either reform or revolution. Policy-makers usually act as a result and in the midst of such situations. To paraphrase Marx, decentralized, unrequited violence is frequently found in the role of indispensable midwife to *reform*. To advocate reforms in Latin America without tolerating, accepting and sometimes even welcoming and promoting the only kinds of pressures which have proven to be effective in getting reforms through is to risk being accused of hypocrisy and deception: now that the United States has declared itself in favor of a variety of reforms in Latin America, it should perhaps be apprised of the circumstances and hazards usually associated with such an enterprise.

Crisis as an Ingredient of Reform

From violence we now move on to a more general concomitant of reform, namely, crisis. Violence is frequently an important cause and a conspicuous element of a crisis situation (a) because the fact of violence shows that a serious problem exists that requires immediate action, and (b) because the violence itself is felt as dangerous by the constituted authorities who will act to suppress it directly.

Crisis has been defined as a "situation in which there is a great stress toward action, toward the resolution of conflict"[16] and, we

---

[16] H. D. Lasswell, "Attention Structure and Social Structure" in *The Communication of Ideas,* Lyman Bryson, ed., Harper, New York, 1948, p. 262.

might add, toward the solution of problems. The reasons for which a developing emergency or crisis is favorable to problem-solving have not received much attention perhaps because the matter seems so self-explanatory. "Crisis concentrates attention," says Lasswell,[17] and it may well be that some problems simply fail in ordinary times to get attacked effectively, not for lack of knowledge, nor even for lack of motivation, but simply for lack of attention. Experience also shows that crisis may make it possible to take required actions against powerful groups which are normally well entrenched and invulnerable; finally, crisis may stimulate action and hence learning on a problem on which insight has been low and which for that very reason has not been tackled as long as it was in a quiescent state.

Yet, can we take it for granted that crisis-induced anxiety about a problem will help insight? Psychological findings hardly permit us to be confident in this regard. Experimental evidence rather appears to indicate that the injection of pressure and tension is not at all certain to improve performance in problem-solving activities. It apparently helps to speed up routine tasks, but turns into a hindrance with problems whose solutions require reflection and insight.[18]

How can the apparent contradiction between the findings of the psychologists and the commonplace attitude of the politician who relies on crisis to produce solutions be resolved? To a large extent by showing that in this case, as in many others known to economists, propositions about individual behavior cannot be extended uncritically to society at large, however suggestive they may be.

In the first place, it is easy to understand that, in a nation, the

---

[17] *Ibid.*, p. 262.

[18] "Results have indicated that the quality of performance in complex learning situations is inversely related to the subjects' degree of anxiety." I. E. Farber, "Motivation in Verbal Learning and Performance," *Psychological Bulletin*, V. 52, 1955, p. 323. For a cautious summary of experimental results, see Kenneth W. Spence, *Behavior Theory and Conditioning*, Yale University Press, New Haven, 1956, Chapter 7. The following is a very strong statement intended by the author, a psychologist, for generalization to societal problem-solving situations: "The basic psychological notion here is that, beyond some optimum level for facilitation, increased motivation serves not only to energize the organism but also to restrict its capacity to select among alternatives at all levels of behavioral organization. The result is that heightened emotion and drive tend to produce stereotypy . . . [which] reduces capacity to solve problems . . . A normally intelligent raccoon trying to get out from under a stinging shower will persistently bang its head against a locked door that used to be open, completely ignoring free passageways to left and right." Charles E. Osgood, "Reciprocal Initiative," in James Roosevelt, ed., *The Liberal Papers*, Anchor Books, New York, 1962, p. 190.

quantity of decision-making, i.e., the total motivation to act, will be increased as a result of the intensification of the problem: certain decision-makers will pay attention to 50 per cent inflation when they were not particularly disturbed by 10 per cent inflation; more important, new dangers or problems — loss of elections, revolution, secession — arise as a consequence of the aggravation of the old problem and some decision-makers will be sensitive to these threats when they were indifferent or opposed to proposed actions on the problems of land tenure, inflation or Northeastern backwardness as such. In other words, new, hitherto indifferent or hostile forces will join to support actions, hence new alignments become possible and the possibility of new moves is perceived. All of this has no counterpart in individual problem-solving.

But what about the *ability* to solve problems, or the *quality* of this quantitatively augmented decision-making? Is there any reason to think that the intensification of the problem will tend to raise the level of insight? In this regard, we can have no certainty and the findings of the psychologists may well hold: we may merely get a spate of decision-making more or less in line with "the state of the arts," i.e., with whatever views are already held at the time about the way in which the problem should be tackled. And since the very fact that we had to wait for widespread violence to take any action makes it likely that insight into the problem is at a low level, such decision-making may not improve matters very much.

Yet, here also the parallel with individual problem-solving can be misleading: in experiments on individual problem-solving, anxiety is injected artificially from the outside while the problem itself remains the same whereas in societal problem-solving, anxiety is induced *by a change, an aggravation of the problem itself,* and frequently this very aggravation makes it possible to understand it better. For example, as inflation accelerated in Chile from the 20 per cent rate of 1939–52 to the 50–90 per cent rate of 1953–55 it became quite clear, as one commentator put it, that wage and salary increases in line with escalator clauses could not be financed out of profits but were bound to lead to further inflation. Similarly, each successive drought in the Northeast brought out one or several ways in which preceding efforts at strengthening the region's resistance to the scourge had gone awry. The 1958 drought, for example, highlighted and exposed the drastic decline in both technical competence and ethical standards which had been suffered by the agency (DNOCS) traditionally in charge of drought relief and public works in the area; this experience was partly responsible for the establishment of a new agency (SUDENE) with a different approach and organization.

The intensification and aggravation of a problem, frequently accompanied and signalled by certain forms of violence, is therefore one way in which reformers strengthen their own motives, gather new allies and gain new insights. Frequently it will not be possible to distinguish clearly which came first, the new motivation, the new allies or the new insights. The appearance of potential new allies will make the reformmongers change the character of their reform proposals so as to accommodate those allies and the emergence of new ideas leads to a search for groups that may support them.

In spite of the fact that this interplay opens up a wide range of possibilities, one particular way of contriving reform holds a privileged place in the popular imagination: the perception of common dangers resulting from the aggravation of the problem is expected to bring the warring parties "to their senses" and result in an equitable solution of the problem "just in time," i.e., just as the revolution was about to take over. Reformers are in this case counting on the danger, the crisis, the emergency, the "brink" to panic everyone into action and their expectations are rather similar to those of revolutionaries: for the latter, the problem is solved by jumping over the brink into an unknown but that much more "transparent region"; for the reformers, the look down the brink is to lead to national reconciliation and rededication through which the overdue reforms are consummated and the problem is finally solved. Both conceptions characteristically assume that a total solution exists, but is sabotaged and held back, either by the "ruling class" which must be destroyed or by misunderstandings, inertia, selfishness and "politics-as-usual" which must be swept away in a great movement toward national union. The idea that national union born out of national emergency is sufficient to solve the country's problems in a comprehensive and integrated fashion is almost as tenacious and powerful a myth as that of "total" change via revolution.

The myth is constantly invoked by policy-makers of every kind, but in only one of our studies did reform or important policy decisions come about approximately in this way. In Colombia in 1960, after renewed concern about unrest and the heritage of violence in the countryside, an attempt was made to bring together all factions of opinion for the purpose of formulating an agrarian reform project once preliminary statements by party leaders had shown a convergence of opinion on the subject. Yet even here "politics-as-usual" was resumed in short order so vigorously that the Agrarian Reform

Bill, elaborated in the fall of 1960 by a special non-partisan National Agrarian Committee, was bitterly fought in Congress by the opposition, found itself in serious jeopardy several times and had to be considerably watered down before it was finally approved in December 1961.

If we look at the important decisions that were taken in the fight on inflation in Chile or the establishment of SUDENE in Brazil, we find even more that they were marked by bitter and protracted battles, unexpected switches, and narrow margins of victory rather than by the miracle of sudden national unanimity. The reason is precisely that situations do not suddenly change from normal to emergency or crisis. Rather, we have here a gradual ascent in the course of which a *succession* of new reform ideas and possible alliances come into view. Besides, there is always disagreement among different groups as to how serious the crisis really is. Even the kind of violence so noticeable in Latin America, being decentralized and unrequited, does not create immediately a situation of utter emergency, but can rather be compared to what is accomplished in the United States by the sending of protest mail to the White House.

Thus, storms and emergencies gather for a long time and various groups in turn become alerted and sensitized to them gradually and unevenly. Hence, a series of attempts at dealing with the problem through changing coalitions is more likely than a Unique Comprehensive Reform.

This conclusion is strengthened by the fact that a problem such as land reform is in fact a collection of problems each of which is likely to fascinate a different clientele: those who favor, say, aid to progressive farmers in the form of tax incentives are not likely to be the same as those who wish idle estates to be broken up. By combining such measures into a "comprehensive" program, one frequently risks combining the enemies of both into a majority of the decision-makers. In Colombia the former measure was taken in 1957 under one government, and progress was achieved on the latter in 1961 with a quite different combination of political forces.

The Emergence of New Problems as an Aid to Reform

Moreover, Colombia, Chile and Brazil obviously faced other issues besides the ones we chose to analyze. What does this mean for the possibilities of contriving reform on "our" problems? A first thought could be that, since the energies of decision-makers are limited, the raising of other problems is bound to distract them and to hold back action in the areas of our special interest. However, this kind of distraction, or substitution of one problem by another, is not at all conspicuous in our stories unless one considers the lack of action on our three problems during the second World War as an instance.[19] To the contrary, the arising or aggravation of an "extraneous" second problem B is frequently seen to help decision-making on problem A, as though action on A were stimulated not only by its own intensification but also by the injection of any new concern.

One way in which such reinforcement can happen is through the familiar mechanism of logrolling. The advocates of land reform might enlist additional support for their project from, say, the advocates of urban low-cost housing projects by promising to support the latter cause by their vote and influence. There is evidence of this kind of mechanism in the story of Brazil's Northeast. We noticed that Kubitschek's support of the SUDENE project was not unrelated to the support for Brasília and Kubitschek's expansionary monetary policies on the part of the SUDENE backers. Inversely, President Epitacio Pessôa attempted to placate opposition to his large-scale spending in the Northeast by undertaking railroad and other projects in the Center-South as well.

Another type of coalition-building is more prominent in our empirical material. It arises not when two problems merely coexist and the backers of reform trade their votes, but when one problem is seen to be interrelated with the other so that to solve or attenuate one is expected to improve the other. If this can be shown to be the case, the backers of one reform will support the other *in their own interest* rather than merely in the expectation of having the favor returned to them.

A good example of this way of acquiring new allies is the junction of the land tenure and the balance-of-payments problems in Colombia. Ordinarily those who are interested in improving the conditions of the peons and their access to land ownership or secure tenure are entirely distinct as a pressure group from the officials in the Central Bank and the Ministry of Finance who are concerned with the balance of payments. But since balance-of-payments improve-

---

[19] This may be so because the three problems we have analyzed have all been crucial, dominant problems in their respective countries at least during certain periods. A dominant problem could be defined as one that holds back action on a series of other problems because of the general expectation that the latter will largely vanish once the dominant problem is solved. The chapter on inflation in Chile quotes a particularly clear, if naïve, illustration of such alleged dominance (p. 215).

ments (smaller imports or larger exports of agricultural products) can presumably be realized through better land use we have a potential community of interests between the two groups which came to the fore in Colombia when the country faced a difficult balance-of-payments problem after the end of the Rojas Pinilla regime in 1957. One of the more important steps in the sequence of policy-making around the land problem (Decree 290 of 1958)[20] can largely be traced to this confluence. Thus new allies are secured not only by the aggravation of the central problem which is the target of reform but also by the aggravation of another problem, if it can be plausibly argued that the cure of the latter is connected with that of the former.

The Northeast of Brazil provides us with another, somewhat more complex instance of this relationship. The natural claimants for federal aid to the Northeast were of course the political representatives of the area itself. They traditionally secured the appropriation of relief funds and were responsible for the establishment of the first federal agencies and for the large public works programs in the area. But in the late fifties an interest arose in reorganizing and reorienting these agencies and programs. This move had only limited support in the Northeast since it was directed against some of the local power-holders. But at the same time the apparent inefficiency of the way in which federal funds had long been spent in the Northeast led to concern *outside* of the Northeast. And on the basis of this interest, Northeastern reformers were able to build a coalition with groups in the Center and South. The problem of waste of public funds in the Northeast mobilized groups quite different from those who were traditionally the advocates of federal subsidies to the region. But support of the former groups became most valuable when an attempt was made to attack the Northeastern problem through new approaches which were opposed by a number of traditional Northeastern interest and pressure groups.

The possibility of solving local and regional problems by mobilizing forces outside the region is of particular interest to the reformer who wishes to attack problems by methods short of revolution. When, within a sovereign country, the pro-reform and counter-reform forces are solidly arrayed against one another and the latter are solidly entrenched, it may well be difficult to achieve reform without resort to revolutionary violence. But if the same situation is characteristic of a region within a country, the reform forces can form alliances with

[20] Decree 290 required the cultivation of minimum percentages of land, according to quality of land. Ed.

groups outside of their region and overcome in this fashion the local diehards. This freedom to maneuver serves to offset two important disabilities under which regional reform movements labor: the threat of revolution is not available to them since they cannot seize the central seats of power and the threat of secession is usually none too credible.

Reformers would do well therefore to be on the lookout not only for symptoms of aggravation of their own problem. By keeping a watch for the emergence of other concerns they may well be able to pick up new allies and to dispense with some old ones who are no longer available or wanted.

The Switch to the Antagonistic Perspective

As we survey the successive attacks on our problems, as well as the many proposed measures, remedies and solutions, the distinction between measures perceived and intended as either antagonistic or non-antagonistic provides us with one way of organizing that plentiful and seemingly disparate material. Do our country studies give us any clue about the sequence in which each category makes its appearance? Does this sequence depend exclusively on the political situation or also on the evolution of the problem itself?

Such questions are of particular interest to reformmongers, for reform, if conceived as an alternative to revolution, is not just any attack on a problem but one that has at least some antagonistic content: the power of hitherto privileged groups is curbed and the economic position and social status of underprivileged groups is correspondingly improved.

It may be helpful, before entering into this matter, to set out schematically the varieties of conceivable policies or events to which the antagonistic or non-antagonistic label might be attached. The policies or events shown in the cells of the table are purely illustrative and are drawn from our studies. For example, land tax schemes, a mildly antagonistic measure, belong in the third column because they affect landowners adversely, and in the second row because the landless peasants do not perceive them as immediately beneficial to them. Thus they are distinguished from expropriation (first row, third column), that antagonistic measure par excellence, which simultaneously hurts the rich and benefits the poor. The other conceivable varieties of antagonistic outcomes — those that hurt the poor while benefiting or leaving indifferent the rich — are never actually advocated; but they happen, as when during an inflation or a drought the rich get richer and the poor poorer. In the following discussion we shall have occasion to refer to most of the possible policies shown in the table.

One striking observation which emerges from our studies is that frequently the horizon of policy-makers seems to be limited to either antagonistic or non-antagonistic remedies to the near exclusion of the other. Policy-makers act typically as though they were either completely oblivious of the possibility of redistribution of power and wealth or completely fascinated by it. Not that all policy-makers, after having long dealt in non-antagonistic remedies, suddenly favor antagonistic measures; but these measures suddenly "steal the show," become the dominant theme around which conceivable solutions of the problem are discussed. The situation reminds one of the well-known psychological experiments where a subject is shown a composite picture in which he perceives either an elegant woman or an old witch (or: either seven or eight cubes) and can perhaps learn to switch from one to the other and back, but can never perceive both together.

Now, to a considerable extent, the change in outlook which makes people suddenly switch from, say, a non-antagonistic to an antagonistic perspective is tied to general political and historical developments. No doubt the Cuban revolution contributed powerfully to placing the land reform issue in its most antagonistic form on the agenda of Latin American policy-makers. But, while such overriding influences must be recognized, an exploration of the inner dynamics of the problem-solving process can give us a fuller understanding of such switches in perspective.

Take, as a particularly clear example, the droughts in Brazil's Northeast. Here is a natural calamity gravely affecting all the people making their livelihood in a certain region, and among possible remedies thought will quite normally be given first to the securing of relief and investment funds from the rest of the country and to public works which might attenuate the effects of the next calamity and improve the regional economy in general. The region secures a supplement of consumption and investment resources from the outside, and the intention, presumption and general impression are that all major groups in the region will stand to profit in some measure from the transfer. However, as the problem is tackled in this non-antagonistic fashion over a long period and yet remains as far as ever from a satisfactory solution, renewed analysis turns up some antagonistic factors: the differential impact of the drought on the large landowners and the sharecroppers or rural laborers, the enrichment of some groups and the profiteering that come with drought relief and

ALTERNATIVE REFORM POLICIES AND EVENTS ACCORDING TO THEIR
PERCEIVED IMPACT ON DIFFERENT SOCIAL GROUPS

		Impact on the upper-income groups, as perceived by them		
		BENEFICIAL	INDIFFERENT	DETRIMENTAL
Impact on the lower-income groups, as perceived by them	BENEFICIAL	NA Northeast: Allocation of Federal funds. Colombia's agriculture: Special credit facilities and technical assistance.	NA Colonization of public lands.	A Expropriation of privately held lands and parceling out to peasants.
	INDIFFERENT	NA Tax rebates and special credits to large landowners introducing mechanized cropping.		A Land tax designed to force landowner to cultivate or rent or sell.
	DETRIMENTAL	A Profiteering during drought. Ordinary course of events in early stages (especially 1904–07) of Chilean inflation.	A Ordinary course of events during Northeastern droughts.	NA (?) Mutual sacrifices in inflation.

A = antagonistic   NA = non-antagonistic

public works, and, perhaps most important, the impossibility of putting to productive use the waters dammed up in the expensive reservoirs because of the obstacles to irrigation under existing systems of land tenure. Some policy-makers become aware of these factors before others, of course; in fact, in the Brazilian case, we encounter the extraordinarily farsighted and crafty Arrojado Lisboa, the first director of DNOCS, who, just because he realized the antagonistic implications of irrigation, decided to soft-pedal that aspect of the problem and to concentrate on the non-antagonistic task of dam construction in the expectation that, once in place, the dams themselves would "cry out" for progress in irrigation.

Such calculating foresight is rare indeed and generally the various facets of a problem are revealed to the surprised policy-makers, or to some of them, as their labors advance. But if, in a first phase, such labors are entirely concentrated in the non-antagonistic area, and if the problem does contain an antagonistic component, then at some point this component will appear as the principal task. Since antagonistic tasks will ordinarily appear after non-antagonistic policies have long been in use, the attraction of the new is reinforced by the discredit of the older set of policies or perhaps simply by boredom with them. Here lies one explanation for the thoroughness with which non-antagonistic policies may suddenly give way to an antagonistic perspective.

The Brazilian sequence is broadly repeated in our Colombian and Chilean stories: In 1959–60 antagonistic proposals moved to the center of the stage in both countries. In Colombia, the theme of outright land reform became dominant in 1960 after experiments with colonization and land taxation had turned out to be unsatisfactory and after entirely non-antagonistic policies, such as agricultural credit, storage, extension, etc., had long been in more or less intensive use. In Chile, the idea that deep "structural" changes, largely of an antagonistic kind, were required to deal with inflation, rather than "merely" monetary measures that would leave the relative power and income positions of various social groups largely intact, appeared around 1958–59 with the strength of a fundamental new insight.

It could be asked why our stories seem to move primarily from the use of non-antagonistic to antagonistic remedies. Is it because the latter are intrinsically more persuasive? This is hard to believe. The discovery that non-antagonistic remedies are available after antagonistic measures have held sway should in principle be greeted as just as stunning an intellectual discovery as the opposite feat. It requires at least as much imagination and sophistication to perceive that two groups whose interests were universally assumed to be wholly divergent actually have some important interests in common as to notice an opposition of interests between groups that were hitherto thought to be, and thought of themselves as, partners traveling along the same road toward common objectives. To illustrate, we recall the sweeping victory of Free Trade with its doctrine that foreign trade is mutually beneficial over mercantilism's dogma that one trading partner's gain is the other's loss. The similar discovery that Russia and the United States actually share one overriding interest, namely survival, while it has not created international harmony, has nevertheless had a profound effect, not only on the debates about nuclear strategy and disarmament, but on the behavior of the two super-powers as well.

Some elements of our stories can also be quoted here. In Colombia, Currie's 1961 proposal to accelerate industrialization and urbanization was favorably received in some sectors of public opinion largely because it opened up a non-antagonistic perspective, a way of sidestepping land reform and its traumatisms. In Chile during the early fifties, the long-continued, desperate and futile struggle of each group to secure a favored position for itself in the course of inflation endowed with considerable intellectual prestige the idea of "mutual sacrifices." This is a special kind of non-antagonistic remedy (see the table, third row and column): it proposes that all parties undergo an immediate loss, proportionate to their economic position, to solve the problem of inflation; but such a remedy is unlikely and turned out to be particularly difficult to put across.

The difficulty of finding in our material really good and effective examples for a shift from the antagonistic to the non-antagonistic perspective is easily explained. We are dealing with societies where the existing social order had not been seriously disturbed or questioned at the point of departure of our stories. The remedies then proposed were those advocated by the well-entrenched upper classes who had no doubts about the identity of their own interests with those of society at large. Only later was this assumed harmony questioned, and the discovery that an antagonistic treatment might be required came as a blinding insight after so long a period of firm belief in, and practice of, the non-antagonistic therapy. This must be understood if the depth of antagonistic feeling in Latin America today is to be correctly gauged.

The Reformer—Naïve or Wily?

In principle, the turn toward the antagonistic perspective should give their chance to both revolutionaries and reformers. Revolutionaries will maintain, as we have seen, that the needed changes cannot be effected without a *prior* overthrow of the "system"; reformers, on the other hand, behave like the country or the chessplayer who exasperatingly fights on when "objectively" he has already lost — and occasionally goes on to win! The reformer sets out after his reforms blissfully unaware that the ruling class will never allow this or that antagonistic measure to pass or to become effective. He is a naïve and pathetic figure at the start, an easy target for the revolutionary's sarcasms, but since he *acts,* he learns from his mistakes and from the resistances he encounters, and he frequently ends up as a wily individual from whom the revolutionary may well learn a trick or two.

This education of the reformer is well brought out in our stories. In Colombia, for example, reformers attempted in the fifties to

achieve better land utilization through the mildly antagonistic measure of penalty taxation combined with the non-antagonistic measure
of colonization of public lands. But they soon found out that planned
colonization can make at best only a marginal contribution to the
solution of the agrarian problem and that penalty taxation arouses
opposition without generating support, since it is fiercely resisted by
the landowners but is not perceived as a direct benefit by the landless
farmers. The turn to land reform can in part be explained by these
negative experiences; even though it is a more antagonistic measure
than taxation, its proponents are sure of support from the campesinos,
they do not incur the hostility of the small and medium-sized landowners, and the large ones may actually not fight the reform very hard
because any individual owner is liable to think that the reform will
either not be applied at all or will not reach down to him. Taking full
advantage of such constellations, our "naïve" reformer has by now
turned into a master tactician who manages to slip through a work-
able reform to the surprise and dismay of both landowners and
revolutionaries!

A similarly a priori improbable feat is the establishment of SUD-
ENE with its group of determined, reform-minded top officials,
equipped with considerable finance and power, in the middle of a
Northeast still dominated by its traditional elites. Again, this achievement was due to learning from prior non-antagonistic attempts at
solving the Northeastern problem and to a judicious exploitation of a
crisis atmosphere combined with a remarkable talent for forming
temporary alliances.

The reforms which take place in Latin America today are anything but manifestations of sweet reasonableness. Nor are they
accurately described as resulting from a "recognition by the ruling
class that it has to give up something in order not to lose everything,"
as the cliché would have it. Rather they are extraordinary feats of
contriving in the course of which some of the hostile power groups
are won over, others are neutralized and outwitted, and the remaining
diehards often barely overcome by a coalition of highly heterogeneous
forces.

"Divide and reform" tactics are usually found to be one important ingredient of the maneuvers making these feats possible. The
reason why such tactics may be successful has been well put by one of
Latin America's most acute political thinkers:

The social conflicts existing at present in our country express essentially not so much irreducible class struggles as conflicts that divide, within

the domain of each class, its dynamic and static sectors, or the productive and parasitic forces.[21]

When economic development has been underway for some time it may be possible to limit the purely antagonistic portion of one's program to, for example, the "parasitic, reactionary, routine-ridden" landlords while neutralizing and perhaps even enlisting the collaboration of the progressive, modernizing group. This is admittedly an extremely delicate operation both because of the long-standing commitment of the pro-reform forces to comprehensive change and because of traditional fears of property owners that any one reform may be followed by another, more radical one. In fact, at the present time it is still uncertain whether a limited, rather than cataclysmic, reform can be successfully carried out in the Northeast of Brazil where the collaboration of the more progressive cane growers and sugar mill owners is sought in diversifying agriculture in the coastal belt or in Colombia where the reform law tends to exempt efficient large-scale producers from the projected land redistribution.

These considerations qualify our earlier remarks on the way in which action on a problem is stimulated. No doubt this happens most regularly as a to-be-remedied condition is aggravated or intensified. The histories of the Chilean inflation and of the Northeastern droughts abundantly illustrate this point. Yet, under certain circumstances, the opposite relationship will also be found: action of either a reformist or a revolutionary nature may be stimulated when the problem begins to *recede!* In recent years the most conspicuous example of this relationship is the fight against colonialism which has increased in ferocity the more clearly colonialism was seen to be doomed. Action intensified because the task to be accomplished by the anti-colonial forces suddenly looked manageable and a favorable outcome of their fight appeared probable. Similarly the generalized fight for agrarian reform in Latin America today may have been stimulated by the fact that old-style latifundismo has not only been eradicated in the countries which have experienced agrarian revolu-

---

[21] Hélio Jaguaribe, *O Nacionalismo na atualidade brasileira,* Instituto Brasileiro de Estudos Brasileiros, Rio de Janeiro, 1958, p. 50. For a further systematic development of the theme of increasing differentiation of Brazilian society, see his recent *Desenvolvimento econômico e desenvolvimento político,* Editôra Fundo de Cultura, Rio, 1962, particularly pp. 169 ff: Differences in the rigidity of class barriers and traditional power structures in Brazil are also stressed by Celso Furtado in "Brazil: What Kind of Revolution?," *Foreign Affairs,* April 1963, pp. 526–535. [Reprinted in this volume on pages 32–41. Ed.]

tions but is being eroded elsewhere as well.[22] In Colombia, as we have seen, modern commercialized and mechanized agriculture has been expanding in some erstwhile latifundio while others continue to be broken up by spontaneous colonization and squatting. Thus the problem has become smaller and more manageable: in a way, the animal is already cornered and wounded and the agrarian reformers, as elsewhere the anti-colonialists, are moving in for the kill. In such a situation, the reformers do not face a wholly hopeless task, and what would have required a major social upheaval thirty years ago may be achieved today by methods short of revolution.

Action is actually stimulated when a problem recedes, not only by the fact that it begins to look more manageable and "lickable," but also because revolutionaries are likely to redouble their energies when they notice that the problem on which they had counted to revolutionize society is fading away. Lenin had exactly this reaction in the face of the transformation of Russian agriculture consequent upon the Stolypin reforms and was clearly worried lest the land measures "so transform the countryside that it would no longer be a revolutionary force."[23]

In fact, it is quite possible that revolutionaries have one of their best chances when some policy-makers begin to convince themselves

[22] A counter-example that comes to mind is "poverty in the affluent society." Action on the problem of poverty, once it has shrunk in size, becomes more difficult as the remaining poor tend to belong to a *hard core* of sick, old, "unemployable," etc.; action also becomes less compelling because the problem victims are increasingly scattered or isolated. Whether action on a problem is stimulated or slackens as the problem recedes may well depend on these two questions: (1) Does the problem have a hard core? (2) Are the remaining victims of the problem capable of joint action?

[23] Bertram D. Wolfe, *Three Who Made a Revolution*, Beacon, Boston, 1948, p. 360. The following passage quoted by Wolfe (*ibid.*, p. 361) from Lenin's writings is revealing:

"The Stolypin Constitution and the Stolypin agrarian policy mark a new phase in the breakdown of the old, semi-patriarchal and semi-feudal system of tsarism, a new movement toward its transformation into a middle-class monarchy. If this should continue for very long periods of time . . . it might force us to renounce any agrarian program at all. *It would be empty and stupid democratic phrase-mongering to say that the success of such a policy in Russia is 'impossible.' It is possible!* If Stolypin's policy is continued . . . then the agrarian structure of Russia will become completely bourgeois, the stronger peasants will acquire almost all the allotments of land, and agriculture will become capitalistic . . ." (My italics.) *Proletarii*, April 29, 1908, reprinted in *Collected Works*, Third Russian Edition, Vol. XII, p. 193. This passage also shows Lenin to be far less dogmatic concerning the possibility of reform than today's "Marxist-Leninists."

that the problem is well on the way out and that it can safely be left to fade away. This may happen either because, as outsiders, the policy-makers do not experience the problem in their everyday lives or because they are not interested in policies that "merely" help existing trends along instead of majestically initiating new ones.[24] Thus they will judge that patience is in order at precisely the time when those who do experience the problem will become desperately impatient. Interestingly, patience of the outsiders and impatience of the insiders increase for the same reason, namely, that "the end is in sight."

Much has been made in the preceding pages of the opportunity to gain new allies which becomes available to today's reformmongers in Latin America. But even with those allies, the margins with which the battles for reforms are won are narrow indeed. It is therefore easily understood why reformmongers dare not cut themselves off from any actual or potential group support of substantial size even though they may disagree with the final objectives of that group. Clearly it would be foolish for them to gain allies on the Center and Right at the cost of losing the Left.

This need to spread his net as wide as possible will make the reformmonger appear to be quite naïve once again, this time about the dangers of Communist infiltration. Often this is so because the most effective reformmongers are to be found amongst erstwhile revolutionaries who notice, much to their own surprise, that some of the social changes they have been seeking can be achieved without that "prior" revolution in whose necessity they had long believed. To turn such private insights into the collective experience of a group that has long remained in a position of pure protest against the established order is perhaps even more important than the achievement of any single reform in itself if Latin American societies are ever to become "integrated." From this point of view also, the effective reformmonger must delay as long as possible, and perhaps avoid altogether, any break with his radical followers. Frequently this will not require any special effort or dissimulation on his part since he is himself still doubtful — quite rightly so until the returns are in — that it is possible to dispense with revolution.

At his best, our reformer-revolutionary will therefore retain the trust of his old followers even as he enlists aid and support from new quarters. He will now have to play to several quite different galleries; he will contrive change by negotiating for new allies while not ceas-

[24] See p. 154 for an episode in our Colombian story which invites this interpretation.

ing to agitate for it. These two tasks are of course so different that they are best performed if they can be dealt out to *several* principal actors who feel quite independent of each other, in the manner of the struggle for Italian unification which was able to draw on the highly diverse talents of Cavour, a master contriver, and of Mazzini and Garibaldi, who filled the roles of conspirators and agitators. But sometimes there is only one chief actor who, to be successful, must combine both roles, appear in the guise of Necker and Stolypin one day and in that of Danton or Lenin the next — a highly risky assignment, though perhaps also rather an entertaining one!

In fine, the roads to reform are narrow and perilous, they appear quite unsafe to the outside observer however sympathetic he may be, *but they exist.* Having become acquainted with their twists and turns throughout this book, we emerge with a heightened consciousness of the difficulties facing Latin American policy-makers; but also and foremost, with a new appreciation of the many unsuspected and unorthodox opportunities for maneuver and advance.

GUNNAR MYRDAL

Planning in the Underdeveloped Countries*

GREAT poverty is a paramount fact in the underdeveloped countries. Most of them are poorer and less developed than Russia was before the revolution. They are often poorer than the Western countries ever were, even in pre-industrial time. This is particularly true of the most populous among them, which weigh heaviest in any comparison.

For many reasons which I can only mention here — reasons related to the climate most of them must cope with, their social

* Selection from *Beyond the Welfare State*, Yale University Press, 1960. Reprinted by permission of the Yale University Press.

stratification and prevalent valuation schemes, trends in their population development, their greater difficulties in acquiring capital from abroad, their trading position in the world, and the very much greater magnitude of their development problems, due to the fact that they cannot rise like islands in a surrounding of underdeveloped regions — an objective analysis of their situation will for most of them yield the conclusion that they are not likely to develop in a way similar to the historical pattern established by the Western countries. Indeed, it is unlikely that they will develop much, or at all, if the state does not from the outset take a much bigger responsibility for engendering development than was taken by the state during the industrial revolution in the Western countries. There, . . . industrialization was mainly the outcome of a cumulative process of spontaneous growth nourished by the enterprise of individual profit-seekers, exploiting new techniques to their own advantage.

To some extent, the idea of economic planning which is now spreading in the underdeveloped countries is in the nature of a rational inference from their urge for development and from their knowledge of the adverse circumstances in which they find themselves. The contemporary world is also a very different one, providing a very different set of ideological impulses. Since their industrial revolution a hundred or more years ago, the Western countries have travelled a long way towards economic planning along a path which I have traced in the previous chapters. And the economic planning by the monolithic and totalitarian state in the Soviet countries also provides a pattern which, in one respect, is the more relevant, in that most of those countries are, or recently were, underdeveloped themselves, and as, in general, their planning has produced very conspicuous development results. Quite aside from any ideological influences from the Soviet countries, however, the fact that the underdeveloped countries are bent, as the Western countries were not, upon applying planning in the initial stage of underdevelopment, gives it a very different character which, indeed, shows a similarity to Soviet planning.

By the very logic of the underdeveloped countries' situation, planning becomes programmatic in its approach. It does not, as in the Western countries, force itself upon a national community through a gradual process which finally results in a *fait accompli,* while the community often still remains largely unwilling to accept planning as an idea. In the underdeveloped countries, the idea precedes its realization. As economic development cannot be expected to come by itself, planning becomes a pre-condition for development, not, as in the Western countries, a later consequence of development and all the other changes which accompanied it. The underdeveloped countries are thus compelled to undertake what in the light of the history of the Western world appears as a shortcut.

All this follows as a consequence of the fact that planning is being applied at an earlier stage of development, and of the further fact that their conditions for development are so much worse that this seems rationally motivated. It is also a part of the logic of the underdeveloped countries' situation that their programmatic planning should be comprehensive and complete, not pragmatic and piecemeal as in the Western countries. In principle and in theoretical approach, planning anticipates public policies. It does not grow out of the necessity to coordinate such policies as have already been initiated.

There is as yet, of course, very little planning in any of the underdeveloped countries. Even India, which has come farthest in planning, has rightly been characterized as a "functioning anarchy." None of these countries is even approaching the level of planning and overall economic state control which is common in all the Western countries. But an idea is also a reality. It is part of the political dynamics in all the underdeveloped countries that this idea is spreading, and that it, differing from both the ideologies and the facts of planning in Western countries, implies a programmatic and comprehensive state direction of the economic development. In this sense, the attempts at planning in the underdeveloped countries, however little has, as yet, come of them, are more akin to the planning accomplished in the Soviet world.

The Legacy from the Western World

Another major political fact is, however, that the underdeveloped countries outside the Soviet orbit want to plan democratically for development. In any case, they are not prepared to accept the totalitarian and monolithic state as a pre-condition for planning.

They have all defined their goals for state planning in terms of the modern democratic Welfare State of the Western countries. This is particularly true of the countries in South- and South-East Asia, which until recently were colonial dependencies of West-European powers. But it is on the whole true also of underdeveloped countries everywhere else outside the Soviet orbit. The modern Western ideals of economic progress, full employment, social security, equalization of opportunity, wealth and incomes, and in the recognition of the responsibility of the state to form its policies so that these ideals become attained, are often written into the constitutions when these are new. They are everywhere propounded in the introduction to planning documents and official reports on major social and economic problems, and are constantly expressed in declarations by political personalities and intellectual leaders and, of course, in party programs. They are the official ideals. Many underdeveloped countries are eager to have stressed that they are "Welfare States." The fact that the ideals are so very far from realization seems to provide a reason to have them preached at every available occasion, and then usually in more absolute terms than is customary in the Welfare States of the rich democracies in the Western world.

Though it may sound paradoxical, this similarity of purpose represents a fundamental difference between the underdeveloped countries and the Western countries, if that comparison is made in the way which is the rational one from a development point of view: *viz.*, as between the present situation of the former group and the situation of the latter group at that time when they managed to lift themselves from underdevelopment. If the under-developed countries — supported, incidentally, by the entire world — now conceive of economic development as a political issue and the responsibility of the state, and if they define development in terms of a rise in welfare of the masses of the people, it is, so far as underdeveloped countries outside the Soviet orbit are concerned, an entirely new thing in history.

There is a similar and equally fundamental difference in the ideological line followed out in building the political power basis for this "state" which is supposed to accomplish the planning for development towards these goals. The Western countries, at the time of the industrial revolution, had consolidated nation-states, built upon the rule of law, and often including a functioning parliamentary system of representation — in both respects they were, as a rule, much farther advanced than the underdeveloped countries are today. But they were not democracies in the modern sense of the word. Suffrage was generally restricted by income qualifications to a small minority of the people. Only now has full democracy with universal suffrage been attempted successfully without prior attainments of a fairly high level of living and a high degree of equality of opportunity.

The principle of universal suffrage, however, was accepted in almost all underdeveloped countries, and particularly in those which were newly liberated. It was accepted as if it were the only natural thing to do — and as if there were no alternatives. In many of these countries with large illiterate populations, rigid caste and class divisions, and religious or ethnic chasms, democratic rule is prevented from operating, or its realization is delayed. There has recently been a trend in large parts of the underdeveloped world towards military dictatorships of one type or another. In countries where regular elections are held, they are often either rigged or the people are not awakened, informed and organized enough to follow out their interests. Large-scale corruption, nepotism, and petty intrigues for personal power and loot are fairly common and tend to decrease both the efficiency and the prestige of the political and administrative systems. It is a spreading idea that the underdeveloped countries need a "guided" democracy, a "real" and not a "formal" democracy, one that is founded upon consensus and not party struggle, etc. The meaning of these terms is usually left in considerable obscurity, but their general leaning is towards some form of authoritarianism in greater or lesser degree.

But the principle that the power emanates from the whole of the people and that poor and rich alike should have an equal voice in decisions of public policies is established and entrenched. Moreover, the very apparent shortcomings in the political set-up of the underdeveloped countries where democracy is faltering are generally such as to exclude the Soviet type of efficient totalitarian and monolithic regime — except after a possible communist revolution which would take them out of the orbit which I am here discussing.

Therefore, while the underdeveloped countries are bound to strive for Soviet-like programmatic and comprehensive planning, their political institutions, and the whole organization of their national communities, will set narrow limits to the possibility of adopting such techniques of planning. The underdeveloped countries which are democratic or are actively striving in this direction are not, of course, prepared to have a totalitarian and monolithic regime; neither are those countries where democracy is faltering or even those which have come under military dictatorships; and even if they were willing, they would not be able to exert the fanatical discipline implicit in the Soviet system.

Aside from this fundamental political inhibition, there is also a difference in their economic institutions. Unlike the Soviet countries, they have not embarked on wholesale nationalization of production; nor have they made state enterprise and collectivization the rule. And they have not organized their foreign trade and exchange relations in the pattern of a state monopoly.

It can be said, and it contains an essential element of truth, that what some underdeveloped countries are now actually attempting, and more are approaching, is to use such elements of the Soviet techniques for programmatic and comprehensive state planning for economic development as are compatible with the absence of a totalitarian and monolithic state and with a mainly private ownership and management of production and trade. The offspring of this crossing is a breed of planning which is as different from the planning which has materialized in the Western countries as it is from Soviet planning.

The sole purpose of this parenthetical reference to the under-developed countries outside the Soviet orbit is merely to present, in necessarily abstract terms, the reasons why economic planning there is different from that of the countries in the other two orbits, and why the differences are fundamental. They stem from the fact that, unlike the Western countries at a comparable stage, the under-developed countries are now attempting to apply planning in advance of development — in order to create the precondition for development — and from the further fact that their political and institutional conditions exclude them from applying the planning methods of the totalitarian and monolithic state in the Soviet orbit.

PART FOUR

THE RESULTS OF REVOLUTION

INTRODUCTION

To a large extent, the readings in this book have dealt with the advisability of nationalist revolutions. East Germany and China have undergone revolutions; following such changes, their governments have adopted policies often resembling those followed by Russia. Substantial changes have occurred in India following independence and in West Germany after the Second World War. Both countries have largely followed western models of development. The comparison of India, China, East Germany, and West Germany by Professors Malenbaum and Stolper helps to bring out the relationship between political ideology and economic progress.

The results of various kinds of revolution have been presented; the final study deals with the results of policy shifts within a given framework. The various policies followed by the Argentine government from 1955 to 1962 are examined in considerable detail in an attempt to determine whether any of the policies are capable of yielding rapid economic development, or whether a revolution is needed to change the framework within which it is hoped that economic development will take place.

Wilfred Malenbaum is Professor of Economics at the Wharton School; his most recent book is *Prospects for Indian Development*. Wolfgang Stolper's latest book is *The Structure of the East German Economy*. Laura Randall specializes in Latin American studies and teaches economics at Queens College.

WILFRED MALENBAUM and **WOLFGANG STOLPER**

Political Ideology and
Economic Progress:
The Basic Question[*]

Ɪɴ the underdeveloped countries — where live most of the world's people — the hope for economic progress now flames with great intensity. The new international capital facilities of the postwar period, the new programs for sharing modern science and technology, the new interest of wealthy lands in progress in the poor countries — all these present the latter with an opportunity to be rid of the poverty and squalor of their material existence. Their eyes naturally turn to the more developed countries for capital and technical knowledge, and for ideas.

The United States and the democratic nations of the West took the postwar initiative in international programs of financial and technical assistance. These countries were confident that their own vigorous progress, under the stimulus of market demand in a free society, would provide a helpful model for expanded rates of economic growth in the poorer nations. Since 1953, however, Russia and its satellites have also played an active role; they now provide a wide range of development assistance to poorer nations — including important politically uncommitted nations like India. Russia's economic history offers a different model, with programed progress in a totalitarian society. Moreover, the Communist lands, focusing attention on their own rates of economic expansion, proclaim their intention to overtake the nations of the West and thus provide unequivocal evidence to the world of how outmoded are capitalist economic systems.

[*] This article was written while both authors were staff members of the Center for International Studies, M.I.T. The present form of the paper reflects the major editorial contribution of Richard W. Hatch of the Center. But the authors alone are responsible for the views presented. From *World Politics*, April 1960, vol. XII #3. Reprinted by permission of *World Politics*.

Since the aspirations of the people in the poor countries as well as the urgings of popular leaders require that these nations pay heed to whatever methods and procedures promise to increase their rate of economic advance, the present competition between democratic and Communist models has inevitably given economic programs for accelerating a nation's growth a significant political dimension. Ideological alternatives are thrust upon the less-developed nations. Even where the ways of totalitarianism are repugnant to leaders and to traditions — as is certainly true in many such lands — domestic political pressures demand an open mind, perhaps an open door.

Leaders in the new and underdeveloped countries are bound to ask: Are totalitarian regimes more adept at initiating a process of continuous economic growth than democratic governments? If the methods of communism do in fact promise a surer or less expensive route to economic well-being, some of these nations, deeply committed as they are to a free society, may also ask: How much more economic progress in five or ten years, say, for how much less freedom? The relevance of these questions is clear. These nations need material progress; they are confronted with alternative roads differentiated on ideological grounds.

These questions may raise no problem for the Soviet policy-maker. He has been given a doctrinaire identification of means and ends. Unwittingly, perhaps, the policy-maker in the West accepts a similar pattern of thought. Preoccupied with the importance of "democratic means," he tends to identify the ends — progress — with his means — the market economy, the private sector, individual freedom of choice. It is necessary therefore to pose the more basic question: To achieve economic progress, must there be a choice of ideologically distinct routes?

I. COMPARATIVE PERFORMANCE

History now provides the material for some judgment on the role of ideology in economic progress under today's conditions. In each of two pairs of comparable lands — India and China, West Germany and East Germany — there is available reasonably documented experience of some ten years of effort to achieve more rapid rates of economic growth from essentially the same starting points. India and West Germany chose paths under democracy; in both lands, government places a high premium upon private property and individual privilege. In East Germany and in China, on the other hand, the methods used can be traced directly to the totalitarian experience of the Soviet Union; in the development effort, as in other aspects of the social order, individual rights are completely subordinated to those of the state.

In 1950 both India and China had per capita incomes of about $50 — lower than in any other large nation. The two countries initiated their development operations at about the same time and from the same type of economic structure. In both, at least 80 per cent of the working force was in agriculture and small-scale enterprise. If anything, India gave promise of greater progress in view of its advantages in basic resources per man, in transport facilities and modern industry, and in training and leadership attributes. Thus, India apparently had greater scope for using its surface water potential and for exploiting the intensive margins of agricultural cultivation. With the same relative efforts, therefore, larger returns could be anticipated in India than in China. So, at any rate, did it seem in the pre-Plan period.[1]

Yet by 1959 per capita gross national product in India was only some 12–15 per cent above its 1950 level, while in China it had expanded to about double the earlier figure. Almost half (45 per cent) of this difference in performance can be associated with the proportionately greater investment made in China; the remaining difference measures the extent to which each additional unit of capital in China was associated with larger flows of current income.

With an initial gross investment ratio just below 10 per cent, absolute real investment in China had increased by 1958 to five times the 1950 level; in India it about doubled. Foreign aid did not explain this difference: indeed, China's investment was more nearly financed from its current output than was India's. Communist methods made possible a relatively large (40 per cent) feedback of new output into China's domestic investment. But India's voluntary performance in this respect was impressive also. During favorable harvest years,

[1] For an analysis of the comparative pre-Plan status and subsequent performance of the two countries, see Wilfred Malenbaum, "India and China: Development Contrasts," *Journal of Political Economy,* LXIV, No. 1 (February 1956), pp. 1–24; and *idem,* "India and China: Contrasts in Development Performance," *American Economic Review,* XLIX, No. 3 (June 1959), pp. 284–309.

marginal savings rates in India may well have exceeded those in China.

The Chinese put more effort into expanding physical output as against services; a larger proportion of new capital was allocated to agriculture and small industry; the degree of utilization of resources, and especially of labor, was increased significantly. Over the whole period, government played a much larger role in economic life in China than in India. And of course, compared with India's, China's producers and consumers had limited freedom of choice — in techniques of production, in final goods for consumption. Greater regimentation in China was accompanied by considerable flexibility on the part of government. In response to actual developments in the economy, relative emphasis was shifted away from the initial concentration on heavy industry, for example. By and large, China's economic progress has been steady. In India, government adheres to models of growth which are permissive; comparatively few restraints are imposed on individuals whose usual ways of life did not in the past generate economic expansion. There have been impressive spurts of industrial output in India's essentially private modern industry sector, as well as some record crops in years with favorable monsoons. The total performance has been less even; the degree of plan fulfillment has not increased steadily, for example.

In prewar years, East and West Germany constituted an historical, cultural, and economic whole. Their labor and other factor endowments were quite similar; their industrial and agricultural establishments were comparably modern and efficient. While actual output per man showed a slight margin for the western half of the country, there was probably little difference in the productive potential of the two parts. The west did have a real advantage in its soft coal resources and in the lower cost of water transport and water power facilities. In order to escape the effects of Allied bombings in the west during the war, industry in the east was favored. Later, while the Marshall Plan was pumping funds into West Germany, Russian reparations and levies were exacting a heavy toll — perhaps one-fourth of industrial production — from current output in East Germany. While Allied troops were basically fed from outside, the Russian occupation lived off the land. Still, Russian demands did serve to stimulate output, particularly in coal and potash, in synthetic rubber and gasoline. There is some evidence that East Germany was getting on its feet more rapidly in the years to 1948. Although it still had a significantly lower product per person than West Germany (some 40 per cent lower) in 1950, an objective appraisal suggested that, as of that date, output potential over the next decade, say, could be more rapid than in the west.[2]

West Germany expanded its gross national product about 10 per cent more than did East Germany between 1950 and 1958. In the light of the different roles of the occupying authorities, it is not surprising that West Germany was able to maintain both higher investment and higher consumption levels. More surprising is the fact that the output gain associated with each unit of investment was also greater in the west, despite the opportunities which under-utilized facilities offered East Germany in 1950.

In contrast to West Germany, East Germany focused on heavy industry and self-sufficiency. There was a relative neglect of agriculture and consumer-goods output generally. Emphasis on heavy industries, especially from an uneconomic raw materials base, was costly for an area renowned for its skilled labor and the quality of its machinery output (optics, electrical goods, and fine mechanical products). The rigid system of controls imposed by East German authorities encountered heavy resistance, especially in farm areas. Major difficulties arose in meshing the complex components of a modern industrial system. All this stands in great contrast to a West Germany which gave ready scope to its entrepreneurs by maintaining a predominantly free market. The effects of these alternative approaches are most apparent in foreign trade — of basic importance in both countries. With competitive prices and market incentives, West Germany expanded its international role along the lines of its comparative advantage. Controlled prices, allocation schemes borrowed from Russia, and the inefficient bilateralism of a trade in which three-fourths of the total was dominated by Russia and the satellites meant that East Germany could not realize its industrial capabilities.

The advocates of neither democratic nor Communist methods can find in the experiences of India and China, of West and East

---

[2] For an analysis of the comparative status and performance of the two countries, see Wolfgang Stolper, *The Structure of the East German Economy*, to be published by Harvard University Press. Preliminary results have appeared in Wolfgang Stolper, "The Labor Force and Industrial Development in Soviet Germany," *Quarterly Journal of Economics*, LXXI, No. 4 (November 1957), pp. 518–45; and *idem*, "The National Product of East Germany," *Kyklos*, XII (April 12, 1959), pp. 131–66. A German translation of the *Kyklos* article has appeared in *Konjunkturpolitik*, (West) Berlin, 1959, No. 6, together with two extremely interesting critical discussions by Werner Gebauer, "Eine neue Berechnung des mitteldeutschen Sozialprodukts," *ibid.*, pp. 344–53, and by Bruno Gleitze, "Niveauentwicklung und Strukturwandlung des Sozialprodukts Mitteldeutschlands," *ibid.*, pp. 374–82.

Germany, evidence of a systematic relationship between ideology and the rate of economic progress. Leaders in the underdeveloped lands — and policy-makers in the wealthier nations — cannot expect dogma to bring the growth they seek. Do the two sets of case histories permit a consistent explanation?

II. UNDERLYING FACTORS

By focusing on the technical determinants of economic growth, some light can be thrown upon the apparent paradox. Let us think of the rate of growth as the product of the rates at which output per unit of capital changes and the capital stock itself expands. By committing itself to the achievement of more rapid economic expansion, a government commits itself to change the nation's savings (or investment) ratios and its capital-output rations — usually both. There are alternative courses of action to these ends. And it is with respect to the methods, more than to the ends, that a government's action reflects its adherence to democracy or to communism. Totalitarian regimes can squeeze consumption, or can limit the increases in consumption in ways unacceptable to a government dependent on the ballot box. Thus, at some time in East Germany or China, rationing has been carried to extreme levels; family life has been communalized; a large part of crop production has been procured from the peasantry under pressure at low prices for resale at high prices. While such measures permit larger allocation to investment, it may be noted that under Communist control they also permitted large appropriations to the Soviet Union, as in the case of East Germany. On the other hand, in West Germany, where there was a clear opportunity for gain by the investor, voluntary savings increased rapidly. Even in a poor nation like India, consumption habits did permit very large voluntary savings in years when there was rapid growth in income for the mass of the people.

The capital-output ratios depend upon the economic wisdom in new investment allocation as well as the vigor with which the nation's human resources are applied to already existing capital. We know well that, in free societies, individual motivations have resulted in efficient over-all performance, in large returns per unit of capital. On the other hand, the right of freedom of economic choice scarcely assures such results everywhere. Russia and China provide concrete evidence that the much larger range of centralized economic decisions necessary to achieve progress in a controlled system can be made with effective results. However, this has not always been true either;

indeed, involuntary transfers of savings have been known to generate apathy and even active non-cooperation on the part of the population.

The needed changes in the savings ratios and in input-output relationships can certainly be visualized with democratic as well as Communist methods. These basic parameters have not only economic but psychological and sociological dimensions. Both Communist and democratic regimes will find the new measures more effective if they take cognizance of existing relationships in the society. This is particularly true for democratic nations, which depend much more upon voluntary cooperation and hence upon the existing pattern of motivational forces in the society. Success by Communist methods places upon government the requirement for more action and more perseverance in assuring its fulfillment; success under democracy requires action based on greater insight into the structure of the society and the economy.

These observations can be illustrated in the two sets of countries. Both East and West Germany had relatively modern, efficient, and complex industrial and agricultural organizations. The profit incentive — even modified in some measure by restraints of a government seeking social-welfare objectives — was of tremendous importance for economic performance. The situation in India and China was completely different. Their economies were market-oriented to only a limited degree. Custom and tradition were of pervasive importance in economic activity — especially in rural areas, where most of the population, workers, and even output are centered. Attainment of specific objectives required carefully planned governmental programs much more than reliance upon the price and profit mechanism.

The very different economic circumstances prevailing in the two sets of countries place very different sets of requirements upon governments seeking more rapid economic progress — whether by democratic or by Communist methods. West Germany's faith in the free market made obvious sense; the government's recognition of the need for change permitted it to superimpose a broad and flexible system of fiscal controls, as well as capital allocations, wherever these were necessary to make the nation's resource endowments best serve its economic needs In this free society, state control increased; about half of all investments were directly or indirectly affected by government.

In contrast, East German planners slavishly copied the Russian model, a pattern prepared for substantially different resource endowments than prevailed in East Germany. Steel produced with

Ukrainian iron ore and Polish coal was expensive. In Germany it was exceedingly difficult for government to acquire the know-how for establishing and administrating precise controls. Thus, it is hard to substitute, for example, for the consistent price system which competitive forces can mold. With the currency reforms in 1948, West Germany acquired such a system. In East Germany, it has yet to evolve. Ubiquitous government may long incur the costs of an inefficient combination of resources.

China's ties to a Russian model of rapid, large-scale industrialization did not impede early recognition of the emptiness of industrialization without agricultural advancement in a nation where most people will long remain rural; of the complementarities rather than the competitiveness, of large industry and many types of small enterprises suitable to a heavy endowment of labor. Important deviations from Communist economic lore were soon made in the allocation of large percentages of investment resources to agriculture and the small-scale sector. A form of communal organization was created with continuous and strong guidance and controls to assure the change that the economy on its own could not generate.

The government of India's models of growth are largely derived from the patterns and relationships found in Western capitalist societies; neither the concepts, nor the values, of the multipliers relevant to a market-conscious economy in the throes of expansion are directly applicable in an institutionalized and static society. The major task of rural improvement and growth was placed upon a national community development and extension scheme. While this action recognized the need, especially in the initial years, of injecting into rural India a new force for change, government did not provide the programs with sustained, strong leadership. In modern industry, where the parallels between Western nations and India were greatest, borrowed doctrine was often in conflict with India's own formulation of the needs of a socialist state. India tries to allocate 50-60 per cent of all investment to the government sector while expecting the private sector to produce more than 90 per cent of total product. These contrasting ratios are not necessarily in conflict; but they do demand close scrutiny of day-to-day investment and production developments to assure that the drive to high levels of investment in the public sector does not impede continued performance and expansion in the private sector.

This examination of underlying factors permits an interesting conclusion. The two more successful nations — Communist China and democratic West Germany — operated on the same sets of technical determinants of growth as did India and East Germany. Their relative success was due to the degree to which they geared their development programs to the existing structure of their economies. Cold and objective appraisals were made of the stages necessary to achieve a state of continuing progress from inadequate starting points. Throughout, they demonstrated flexibility in selecting courses of action. Only those were finally adopted in which practice gave promise of the changes needed in savings rates and in technical input-output coefficients. In democratic India and Communist East Germany, on the other hand, governmental operations on these basic parameters have manifested much less objectivity and flexibility. Indeed, India, where growth under democracy demands a greater interplay of new and old relationships in the society, evidenced less of an experimental and flexible approach to its problem of expansion than did China.

III. IDEOLOGY AND ECONOMIC PROGRESS

Thus no simple ideologic-economic relationship exists. The West German performance means that the Communist formula does not contain the essential ingredient to more rapid progress; nor has democracy in a free society provided India with a guaranty of rapid economic achievement. Not only is economic progress not determined by the ideology to which a nation adheres; indeed, it can be most costly for a nation to adhere persistently to doctrines which counter indigenous economic and social relationships.

Whenever doctrine and policy are borrowed, whenever the results of foreign experience are applied, actual experience with them must be subjected to constant analysis. Only such study can indicate the changes needed to achieve effective results — whether these changes be in the knowledge or ideas imported, or in indigenous habit or relationships. It is not an ideology or an economic theory that will bring growth; it is more energetic and imaginative responses to the record as revealed by intensive study. This is especially true for democratic nations which rule out change by force; new programs must take root indigenously.

The growth record in the poorer nations over the past decade can scarcely give unmitigated satisfaction either to the leaders in the under-developed areas or to the policy-makers in the West. At the least, there is still room for great humility with respect to our know-how about the process of growth. The free market and private enterprise may work — as by and large they have under our conditions — but they may also have but limited relevance in the economic and social circumstances prevailing in the poorer lands. West Germany seems to have worked out a compromise between free enterprise and controls which serves its growth needs. There is undoubtedly some composite path which will provide the centralized direction and co-ordinated performance needed in India, consistent with its democratic aspirations. The specific actions to be taken can be deduced only from a full reading of the actual record of the decade. Dogma can give way to hypothesis, certainty to experimentation.

It is such a composite path — well within the extremes of permissiveness and compulsion — which nations seeking economic progress under democracy need to pursue. Given the limited growth achievements of these lands in the past decade, capital-exporting countries will inevitably provide greater assistance. It is high time that major research efforts — perhaps on a joint basis in each developing nation — be applied to discovering the actual bottlenecks which have been hindering that nation's economic expansion. A development program tailored to these specific tasks has a chance of both achieving material progress and nurturing democratic political ideals.

LAURA RANDALL

Economic Development Policies and Argentine Economic Growth*

I

It is something of a mystery why Argentina has selected an intermittent series of orthodox policies which have yielded neither sustained rapid economic growth nor preferred treatment by foreign lenders.

FULANO DE TAL

"**A**RGENTINA is *not* an underdeveloped country!" So most Argentine economists insist. This proud statement was first made about 1900 when Argentina boasted of a then respectable per capita income of $230. It is still heard over sixty years later when the figure has risen only to $350.[1] This is well above the Latin American average, but the growth of real income per capita in the last fifty years has been a dismal $8/10$ of 1 per cent a year. Why is the Argentine economy so stagnant?

When Perón was overthrown in 1955, one might have blamed Argentina's economic ills on the Great Depression and on the decapitalization and mismanagement of the economy under Perón himself. Traditional economic liberals urged — and still urge — that to restore the halcyon years of just before World War I, a drastic reduction of state enterprise, a reliance on "sound" monetary principles, less taxation and government regulation, and no state interference in the traditional agricultural structure is necessary. Perónists reply that the Argentine governments since 1955 have sold out to the capitalist interests; they insist on more state protection for the economically

---

* I would like to thank Professor Carter Goodrich and Professor Fred Bronner for discussions of the topic and manuscript, and my husband, Francis Randall, for considerable editorial advice. Remaining errors of fact or interpretation are, of course, my own.

[1] In 1950 dollars. Because food is more readily available in Argentina than in many countries, "market basket" adjustments are often made that result in an estimated per capita income almost double that indicated here.

123

weak, and more state action to obtain more favorable terms in foreign trade and to promote domestic growth. Still others reject both liberalist *and* Perónist nostrums, and demand a basic restructuring of the Argentine economy to wrench the country's social groups away from their preoccupation with their respective *shares* of power, which so limits economic growth. It is the purpose of this article to review the economic policies of Argentina's governments during the last seven years, and to provide a basis for judging these three views of Argentina's troubles.

II

The rapid transition from an economy apparently stabilized by means of government subsidy to an economy that was governed by market prices was not easy. . . Consumers, accustomed to paying politically determined prices, benefited by subsidies and by exchange controls, naturally protested against a government that cured its financial ills at the cost of the consumers' sacrifices. We were attacked, accused of selling out the national patrimony to foreign monopolies, of condemning workers to hunger while increasing the wealth of cattle owners and of certain large industrialists, of enriching government functionaries through alleged dealings with foreign enterprises. They called us fascists, communists, perónists, and public thieves, according to the circumstances and the political coloration of the adversary. A complete theory was almost elaborated, which consisted of demonstrating that we were sowing social ills in order to justify an extremist social revolution that would be the consequence of our unpopular methods of government.

ROGELIO FRIGERIO
*Nacionalismo, potencias industrias
y subdesarrollo,* 1961.

In some respects Argentina is a semi-developed area that has yet to become a nation. Its various centers were developed separately on the basis of trade with Europe, not each other. The transport and communications networks that are needed to integrate a national economy still do not function smoothly. No recent struggle for independence has forged a nation, and no threatening neighbor inspires national union. Argentina's cultural capital often seems to be Paris rather than Buenos Aires. In the last seventy years immigrants — chiefly from Italy and Spain — have formed twice the share of the population that they form in the United States. And the Argentine melting pot seems to cook *much* less effectively than ours. It is still possible for an Argentine to ask, "What is national about Argentina? The culture of the Diaguita Indians?"[2]

Insofar as Argentina *is* a nation, it is torn by an unusually ugly and intractable set of class struggles and group hostilities. The very development, urbanization, literacy, and articulateness of the Argentines seem to have politicized a very high proportion of the people, and to have exacerbated all their divisions. Argentines as well as Anglo-Saxon visitors have blamed the persistent unwillingness to compromise on the country's Spanish background, the widespread social irresponsibility on the immigration from southern Italy, the tendency toward authoritarianism and militarism on the German element — all these group judgments are widely believed, and so is the chestnut about how the Argentines have no sense of humor.

Personal selfishness and group irresponsibility toward the public afflict the whole world, and they are difficult to measure. Yet in all soberness it seems justified to say that in Argentina more than in most countries social groups tenaciously cling to their acquired situations and vested interests, strive to maximize their own short-run material advantage to the exclusion of larger ends, and insist that all other social groups are doing the same. Much of what has been written about the social deadlock behind the economic stagnation of France under the Third and Fourth Republics applies *a fortiori* to Argentina.

The social and economic effects of all this are dismal. Laws are disregarded when there is no reason to fear punishment. To take a by no means trivial example, passing bad checks is a misdemeanor in Argentina, not a crime, and therefore many people pass bad checks and assume that everyone else does so. Business must often be transacted in cash, which greatly slows economic activity.[3] It

[2] Torcuato S. Di Telia, "Tensiones Sociales en Los Paises de la Periferia," in *Revista de la Universidad de Buenos Aires,* Anō VI, Num. 1, Enero–Marzo 1961, p. 61.

[3] The government's repeated leniency towards those who falsify tax returns or evade paying taxes altogether acts as an incentive toward non-compliance with tax laws. It is estimated that revenue loss due to tax evasion and avoidance is roughly equal to 150 per cent of the taxes actually collected. Because an estimated 25 per cent of all businesses are not registered with the tax authorities, the government has recently announced the introduction of a system of checks on and punishment of tax evasion. As a result, 451,000 delinquent taxpayers appeared to normalize their status with the Revenue Service. Some 245,000

is assumed that office-holders take bribes when they can get away with it, and even honest office-holders can count on being thought corrupt. Many groups seem to favor public policies only if their own *shares* of power and wealth will be increased as opposed to those of all other groups; more absolute increases will not suffice. This seems to make it difficult for an Argentine government to secure a majority coalition behind a change in policy without lying or muddying the issues in contradictory ways before various component groups of a proposed coalition.[4] This increases the general impression that the government is in cahoots with other groups to do one's own group out of one thing or another. . . That path leads to paranoia, and nothing is more common than to remark on the mutual distrust and semi-paranoid atmosphere of Argentine politics.

It would be too simple to interpret Perón's economic policy as sheer revenge on the older establishment, and it would be too simple to interpret Argentine economic policy since 1955 as sheer revenge on the Perónist workers by the current establishment — although neither view is short of supporters in Argentina. It would be only a little too simple to describe recent Argentine history as a heedless scramble for an increased *share* of the national income by all social groups. An economist might tolerate such a heedless scramble if it were an essential element in a period of rapid economic growth — as it was in the United States during the Gilded Age. What is distressing about Argentina is that the scramble has persisted while the growth has not. Against this discouraging background one must trace Argentine economic policy in the last seven years.

III

In Latin America there is a good deal of talk about the need for defending the system of private enterprise. But we seldom ask ourselves how this system works in our region. Can the system work well if indi-

---

of this number had not previously been registered as taxpayers. It is estimated that total receipts gained by normalization will amount to 10.8 billion in taxes; 4.6 billion of this amount was paid in by early January, 1963.

[4] It is against this background of mutual distrust that the normal conflicts between advocates of laissez-faire and statist ideology have taken place. It frequently appears to be believed that economic measures are "moral" in and of themselves, rather than a series of acts having clear technical and social implications. It is possible that an obsession with the "morality" of stabilization plans led to the adoption of programs that were too severe to be practical or enforceable, and that the implausibility of the stabilization plans led to an even greater degree of non-compliance than might have been obtained had more moderate decrees been imposed.

vidual initiative is cramped and restricted as a result of social stratification; if antiquated forms of land tenure deprive large numbers of people of the opportunity to use their initiative as independent farmers? Can the system function efficiently when private enterprise is frequently accompanied by restrictive or monopolistic practices which impair or prevent healthy competition?

We have to give dynamic validity to the system in Latin America through structural reforms. But, if instead of believing in this idea, I had at the back of my mind a dark design to destroy it, I would simply adopt the conservative attitude of letting events take their course, without any attempt to change the present order of things; and I would preach the virtues of allowing inflation to continue at an even faster pace, and from time to time, I would recommend anti-inflationary measures bringing with them contraction of economic activity and serious unemployment.

Then I would sit back and wait for the inevitable social explosion — and I should not have long to wait!

DR. RAÚL PREBISCH
November, 1962

When Perón was finally overthrown in September 1955 by a revolt of his own army, his economic legacy to his country was inflation, shrinking supplies of exportable goods, vanishing of foreign exchange, declining ability to import industrial raw materials and capital goods, and consequently a decreasing rate of economic growth. Anti-Perónists blamed much of this on Perón's pervasive system of controls. The Argentine Trade Promotion Institute (IAPI) held a monopoly over the export of farm products (except wool), and over the import of many raw materials and capital goods. The central bank, a dependency of the treasury, controlled the deposit and lending policies of commercial banks. Transport, communications, and insurance were nationalized. Property seized from Axis nationals during World War II was administered by a state enterprise (Dirección Nacional de Industrias del Estado), as were the oil fields (by Yacimientos Petrolíferos Fiscales). The Army and Air Force owned and operated most of the country's iron and steel works, and produced goods for commercial sale.

To reduce this state economic machine and to restructure the Argentine economy, a detailed study of the economy was needed, with recommendations for its improvement. This was provided in a series of reports submitted by Dr. Raúl Prebisch from October 1955, to January 1956. Dr. Prebisch analyzed Argentine economic ills as follows:

Argentina had sought to increase consumption without sufficiently increasing production. National produce per capita increased only 3.5

per cent during 1946–55, with the result that Argentina, in the effort to increase consumption, resorted to borrowing abroad and letting its industrial plant run down.

This inadequate production in turn was the result of the insufficiency of foreign exchange to pay for imports of fuels, raw materials, machinery, and equipment. Even if machinery were imported, it could not be utilized owing to lack of electric power, while goods produced by the machines could not be transported owing to the deterioration of the transport system.

The weakness of Argentina's foreign exchange position was attributed to insufficient investment in farm production for export, and to the insufficient development of import-substitutes, most notably oil.

Additional mistaken policies included the government's purchase of foreign firms (instead of encouraging the participation of foreign capital), the development of an excessive government bureaucracy, the exchange permit system, and deliberate inflation. Inflation was the result both of wage and salary increases in excess of increases in productivity in a number of sectors of the economy, and of the expansion of bank credit to cover deficits arising from surplus crop disposal, the transportation system, and mortgage credit operations.

Dr. Prebisch urged that Argentina's traditional exports (grain and livestock products) be encouraged by a substantial rise in the prices paid for them, which could be effected by a reduction of the overvalued exchange rates. New exports, especially manufactured goods, were to be encouraged, while imports were to be limited to essential production goods by taxing imports of foreign cars and setting up a system of import priorities for transport and production goods. Argentina was to renounce its nationalist aversion to foreign capital, and obtain funds from abroad to finance the needed imports, especially for the oil industry. It was to consider joining both the IMF and the IBRD, and to avoid deferred-payment arrangements so as to reduce future pressures on the balance of payments.

Dr. Prebisch underscored the need for fiscal improvements. He noted that taxes on consumption had increased from 39 per cent of total revenue in 1946 to 46 per cent in 1955. He wanted to reduce the regressiveness of the tax system and to introduce effective methods of collecting taxes. He hoped to reduce the number of government workers, not by wholesale firings but by not filling vacancies as they arose. Intractable problems, such as the mounting deficit of the increasingly inefficient government transport system, were to await technical studies. With the new military junta in power, Dr. Prebisch apparently did not think it wise to say what was obvious to foreign observers — that the size and cost of the armed forces should be drastically reduced.

Dr. Prebisch submitted his first report on October 24, 1955. Three days later, General Lonardi's junta began to implement parts of it. The first step toward simplifying the exchange system was taken by devaluing the Argentine peso from rates that had been ranging between 5 and 13.98 to the dollar to a new official rate of 18 to the dollar. A fluctuating rate, to be determined by the newly-restored free market, was to apply to certain non-essential imports, invisibles, and capital transactions. Free repatriation of profits earned after June 30, 1955 on foreign capital was authorized — this was to be the step in unblocking $100 million equivalent in profits that had been virtually impossible to remit since 1947. However, a system of exchange taxes, surcharges, and subsidies on essential imports, as well as priorities on imports of machines and equipment for the production of import-substitutes (notably oil), softened the impact of devaluation.

In January 1956 Dr. Prebisch submitted his final report and recommendations, this time to a junta headed by General Aramburu, who had ousted Lonardi for being soft on Perónists. In these documents, Dr. Prebisch proposed that the Argentine central bank be freed from direct control by the ministry of finance. It was to have full power to issue general directives and to supervise the operations of the banking system. Commercial bank deposits, which had been "nationalized" and taken over by the central bank under Perón, were to be returned to the depository banks. The Industrial Bank, under government control, was to become an autonomous development bank. Short-term debts were to be funded on a long-term basis, and the use of the *Cédula Hipotecaria* (mortgage bond), which Perón had suspended in 1946, was to be allowed.

The Aramburu junta began to follow Dr. Prebisch's banking recommendations when it granted technical and administrative autonomy to the central bank in 1956. The central bank was given basic powers of control, including authority to vary the discount rate, engage in open market operations, set basic and marginal reserve requirements, and establish minimum ratios of liquid assets to deposits. Direct controls conferred on the central bank included the power to set minimum and maximum interest rates for commercial bank operations, and ceilings for each individual bank's lending, either over-all or by type of loan.

The junta completed the implementation of Dr. Prebisch's major banking proposals on December 1, 1957, when it established three autonomous government banks. These were the National Mortgage Bank, which was once more empowered to raise funds by issuing tax-free mortgage bonds, by accepting savings deposits, and by other forms of borrowing; the Industrial Bank, which was given responsibility for medium and long-term financing; and the Bank of the Nation, which was to give financial support to agricultural production, and was also to take care of the current needs of commerce and industry. This independent banking system was calculated to be of central importance in curbing inflation and reestablishing the confidence of investors in the Argentine economy.

The second major group of Dr. Prebisch's proposed reforms enacted by the Aramburu junta had to do with foreign trade and investment. A multilateral payments system with nine European countries was established in 1956.[5] A ten-year debt-funding operation covering $500 million of Argentina's debt was initiated with five European creditors and Japan. And Argentina *did* join the IMF and the IBRD.

To develop electric power, the junta denounced existing concessions held by private electric concerns in July 1957, and substituted a new mixed firm composed of private electric companies and the state, which was to buy out the private owners over a ten year period.

The oil industry was promoted by two strikingly different but complementary measures. The junta made subsoil petroleum resources the exclusive, inalienable property of the nation, to be exploited only by the state oil firm, YPF. Existing rights of private companies (mostly foreign) as of May 1, 1958, were to be respected, but new concessions were prohibited. But in July 1958, after the junta had given way to President Frondizi, YPF itself signed a series of contracts with private foreign oil firms.[6] These contracts

[5] Supplementary measures included the granting of permission in 1957 for the remittance through the free market of earnings on foreign investments, up to 5 per cent of invested capital for each accounting year prior to June 30, 1955; minimum support prices for gains provided stimulation of traditional exports. An attempt to favor imports of industrial and electrical equipment necessary for economic development was made by imposing advance-deposit requirements on trucks and automotive parts, and by increased surcharges on passenger-car imports.

[6] The terms form of the contracts included payment for private company services per foot drilled, with adjustments for inflation-caused variations in costs, employment of foreign companies to manage a given area, where the companies are paid their costs plus a "profit" based on production; and production by private companies whole output is purchased by YPF.

were criticized by nationalists because they had been negotiated rather than opened to public bid, and because the government was to pay too much for its oil.[7] In view of Argentina's poor bargaining position, the government probably had to choose between high prices or little oil development at all.

In their two and a half years in power after they overthrew Perón, the generals did much for the Argentine economy. They reformed the exchange system and the banks, stimulated investment from abroad, dismantled much of Argentina's vast economic bureaucracy, and tried to put the remaining government enterprises on a self-supporting basis. But the generals left even more undone in the crucial first years after Perón when the situation was still fluid and they might have effected basic reforms embodying Dr. Prebisch's central recommendations; they did nothing fundamental about Argentine agriculture or taxation and they failed to develop new exports. Dr. Prebisch had called for restraint by all social groups for the sake of national economic development, but both labor and the upper classes seemed to view restraint as a senseless means of letting one's enemy increase his share of power.

In 1956 the junta lifted a number of price controls to please business and the landed magnates, and granted wage increases of 30 per cent–40 per cent to placate organized labor, which initiated a fresh inflationary spiral. Deficits persisted in government enterprises; exchange depreciated, reserves were lost, black marketeering flourished. Like Perón before him, General Aramburu left his country a troubled economic legacy.

IV

"Do unto others before others do unto you!"
DOBU ISLAND PROVERB

In May 1958, Arturo Frondizi of the Intransigent Radical Party won Argentina's first really free presidential election since 1916. While the generals had not tackled such problems as agriculture and taxation on the ground that they were interim officials without authority from the people, Frondizi presumably had been voted such authority. Hopes were high in many quarters at home and abroad.

By the end of the year Frondizi secured the adoption of a new stabilization program. He arranged $329 million in credits from the

---

[7] Opposition was particularly bitter since Frondizi, before his election, had written a book in which he opposed foreign exploitation of Argentine oil.

IMF, the United States, and private banks. He devalued the peso in December. His government promised to reduce inflation by reorganizing the exchange system and eliminating the deficits in government and in state enterprises. This was to entail a single fluctuating exchange rate coupled with import taxes and export retentions, a reduction in the number of government employees, and the raising of transportation fares and the price of gasoline. Except for the export retentions, the new stabilization plan closely followed the short-term recommendations of Dr. Prebisch's reports.

However, an immediate result of the stabilization plan was a scramble by labor and business to maintain and increase their shares of the national income. This led to a spiral of wage and price increases that exceeded the 30 per cent rise anticipated by the government. Temporary export retentions and taxes were imposed to absorb windfall gains accruing to businessmen from the operation of the new exchange system. Nevertheless the burden of the December 1958 devaluation apparently fell on the urban workers — and they universally came to believe so! It was estimated that their living costs increased 47 per cent between December 1958 and April 1959, while their wages went up only 37 per cent. Businessmen, though, were able to raise selling prices by more than the increased cost of imported goods.

By November 1959, the government thought it could safely ease some of the import restrictions. The oil fields produced enough to begin exporting. However, this was partly offset when hoof-and-mouth disease in Argentina and politics in Washington closed the United States market to cured Argentine meat. On balance, the results of the December 1958 stabilization plan after a year of operation were decidedly mixed: foreign exchange reserves increased by $220 million, real gross national product declined, the cost of living increased 114 per cent (!), and the rate of exchange declined from 18 to 70 pesos to a dollar at the end of 1958 to 83 pesos to a dollar at the end of 1959. To prevent a further decline of the peso, Frondizi obtained another $250 million from the United States, Europe, and the IMF.

During 1960, Argentine production almost regained the levels reached in 1958. The rate of inflation was *reduced* to 27 per cent. Frondizi finally attempted to make the tax system more equitable; basic income tax exemptions were increased, and the tax office was reorganized in an effort to improve collections. But one major inequity persisted. Workers continued to have their taxes deducted in advance from their wages, while taxes were not withheld from the various forms of upper class income. As workers were well aware, tax evasion was concentrated in the upper income groups.

The government made some progress in cutting costs. It transferred some of its operations to private owners and reduced its work force by 76,643 people during 1959 and 1960. But expenditures on the armed forces and the railroads remained high. Although credits and investment from abroad increased the reserves of foreign exchange during 1960, it was clear that continued foreign confidence would be necessary.

To increase the rate of economic growth, the government increased bank credit and lowered reserve requirements. To offset any inflationary pressure, the sales tax was raised from 8 per cent to 10 per cent, and a tax of 3 per cent on imports and 2 per cent on exports was imposed. In June 1961, most new government hiring was halted for the rest of the fiscal year (which ends, in Argentina, on October 31). Shortage of funds led the government to pay its suppliers with debt cancellation certificates which could be used in paying taxes — instead of paying them cash! To preserve the peso, Frondizi tried to reduce imports by requiring state enterprises to obtain government authorization for certain foreign exchange commitments.

When he tried to keep private firms from wasting foreign exchange, Frondizi was compelled to tackle the sore problem of the finance companies and the automobile industry. Bank interest rates were controlled effectively; the non-bank finance companies were not, and they attracted an increasing volume of funds by offering higher interest rates on deposits. Automobile firms were the preferred borrowers from the finance companies. An undue share of Argentina's domestic capital resources was thus diverted into automobiles. By 1961 there were twenty-two firms (one for each million Argentines!), all making short-term profits from the backlog of demand for cars, all facing a tight future when the backlog was used up, and all contributing heavily to the drain on foreign exchange, since materials and parts for the automobiles had to be imported. Nor were economists convinced that Argentina needed so many cars at that moment. Other firms complained of a credit squeeze.

In August 1961 the government finally authorized the central bank to regulate the capital, interest, and reserves of the finance companies. It lowered bank reserve requirements again, and permitted an increase in bank credit — to unify the capital market and to secure a larger share of credit for sectors of the economy more productive than autos. At the same time, the government announced that it would require greater use of domestically manufactured auto parts, and that it would levy higher surcharges on imports of auto parts.

Simultaneously pressed by the need for revenue and the need to increase exports, the government now imposed taxes on farm products and now rescinded them. To promote domestic production of goods Argentina imported, and to encourage production outside of Buenos Aires, special privileges were granted to investment in steel, petrochemicals, cellulose, and the Northwestern and Patagonian regions.

After almost three years of these *ad hoc* and often halfway measures (mid-1958 to mid-1961), the Frondizi government had failed to end anxiety about foreign exchange reserves, had failed to halt the increases in the cost of living, and had failed to get the country moving again. Frondizi could not dream of reducing the swollen Argentine military. Instead, he made a climatic effort to reduce the government's huge railroad deficit, which accounted for roughly *one fifth of the government's total expenses, or about 80 per cent of the total deficit!*[8] If allowance is made for the fact that the railroads were supplied with fuel oil at specially reduced prices, that they did not make provision for amortization or for the funds they received from the treasury, and that they paid no taxes, the deficit was probably equal to *nearly half the total budget expenditures!*[9] The political opposition to such proposed rationalizations as ending subsidized freight rates and reducing the inflated "work" force can be imagined.

[8] In fiscal 1960–61, the combined operating deficit and capital expenditure of the railroads were 22,233 million pesos ($268 million) out of a total budgetary deficit of 25,406 million ($307 million).

[9] The nationalization of the British-owned railroads in February 1948 was central to General Perón's program of "economic independence." Although it is arguable that the railroads had to be subsidized in order for them to serve the nation properly, the vested interests involved — rates, and of short hours of work — caused the subsidy to be used primarily to maintain their own positions. Consequently, the railroad deficit became an increasingly large and unjustifiable drain on the national budget, while railroad service and efficiency deteriorated steadily. In 1948 the railroads employed 140,000 persons; by 1961, the number had increased to 213,000, and the average working day on the railroads was only 3 hours. Increases in wages, decreases in productivity, and a decline in traffic volume due to truck competition resulted in a shift from profits of 20 per cent of gross income prior to nationalization to heavy annual losses. Despite the need to correct these unsatisfactory conditions, the political strength of the unions for a long time was great enough to prevent remedial action, especially in view of the uncertain political balance of the government.

As a first step, the government announced, in the spring of 1961, its intention to transfer all railroad catering services to private hands, who would presumably end the featherbedding. Therefore the waiters and train stewards of the San Martín line went on strike. The government threatened to fire anyone who did not return to work in 48 hours. The unions countered with an argument that was central to all rail disputes in 1961 — that the government should not have moved unilaterally to nationalize the railways, but should have consulted the union leaders. Although this strike was called off temporarily, others followed in July and August. To avoid further strikes, the government agreed on August 26 to form a new joint labor-management committee to study the problems and submit recommendations within sixty days. It also agreed that any wage increases would be retroactive to June 1.

In meetings of the joint committee, labor and management failed to agree. The government then unilaterally decided to refuse wage increases, to adopt more rational work rules, and to shut down certain repair yards and other services. The unions insisted that the government had violated its agreement of August 26, and the railwaymen went on strike October 30. The government, aggrieved, stated that it would not negotiate until the strikers went back to work. At the same time, it offered severance-indemnification payments and priority in low-cost housing to railwaymen who resigned from the roads. Some workers applied for the indemnification payments, but the strike continued. The break came when Frondizi went to Europe to obtain increased trade and credits. Acting President Guido asked Cardinal Caggiano to negotiate a settlement, which was reached on December 10.

By and large, the workers won. Labor placed two men on the eight man board that runs the railroads. The enforcement of the government's new work rules was postponed until an agreement could be reached. Wages went up and the government lent workers 80 per cent of the wages they had lost during the strike, providing for repayment in 18 monthly installments to begin in April 1962. The system of severance indemnification remained in force and 54,000 workers were pensioned off with five billion pesos. The government released the workers it had jailed during the strike. The cost of the railway strike to Argentina was estimated at one to two year's railway deficit, to say nothing of the reinforced bitterness of the workers.

The settlement was, in effect, a reestablishment of the pro-labor agreement of August 26, 1961. Labor leaders had imposed that agreement on the government because they mistrusted it, and they went on strike chiefly because they mistrusted the government's observation of that agreement. The government's difficulties in trying to reorganize the railroads exemplified and climaxed its difficulties with its whole stabilization plan. There was no lack of adequate technical solutions for Argentina's economic problems, but the men in the affected sectors had little confidence in their government, and would not trust it to the extent of cooperation, while the government lacked the political strength to ram its economies through against popular opposition.

The railroad settlement provoked the resignation of Economy Minister Alemann, who had stood for "firmness" toward the workers. Since he was also known as a "sound" money man, his resignation, coming on top of the expensive settlement, led to widespread speculation against the peso, and more inflation. The accumulation of economic troubles and distrust led the Perónist workers, who had voted for Frondizi in 1958, to vote for the new Perónist opposition ticket in the congressional and provincial elections of March 1962. The Perónist successes were possible only because Frondizi had gambled on legalizing their party. These capped the many grievances that most of the army factions felt they had suffered at Frondizi's hands, and on March 29 the Argentine army once again overthrew the chief of state. Frondizi's government ended as it had begun, amid worsening economic difficulties.

v

If . . . sacrifice is not made voluntarily, the danger is that everything may have to be sacrificed later as a matter of compulsion.

INC. ALVARO ALSOGARAY

The new military putsch was followed by a startling economic decline. The peso fell spectacularly following withdrawal of central bank support in April 1962, within a few weeks of the coup. The new government soon showed itself unable to provide full employment at home or to pay debts abroad. The familiar list of economic difficulties need not be repeated; Argentina floundered anew in the months after March 1962 and has not recovered itself as of the time of writing (February 1963). Argentines and foreigners have often blamed the latest economic decline on "political instability," i.e., on the putsch and the ensuing factional struggles of the military. Perhaps one should look deeper.

A year *before* the overthrow of Frondizi, Argentines might have looked forward to a smiling economic future. The external value of the peso was temporarily stable; the rate of domestic inflation was declining. Foreign exchange reserves totaled $705 million, and one might have hoped that new foreign investment approvals would continue at a rate of over $100 million a year. Petroleum had expanded significantly, and a basis had been laid on which to expand steel and electricity.

But even early in 1961, Argentina's most promising moment in way over a decade, *the country's over-all economic structure — particularly the foreign exchange bottleneck — the government's pattern of expenditures and its ability to shape the economy,* were all still seriously deficient.

The most striking part of the government's budget was the large share devoted to salaries; in 1959 an estimated *80 per cent* went into wages, chiefly for state enterprises and the armed forces. Under Perón, when much of the army budget was used to operate various industries, this emphasis was economically more productive than it was later when army expenses became more purely military. By 1961 expenditure on the armed forces in a land without foreign enemies served the economic function of a largely unproductive public works program, disguising much unemployment by under-employment. The same could be said of the considerable excess labor force in the bureaucracy and state enterprises.[10]

If part of the sum spent on salaries had been devoted to housing in areas where new projects were located, worker mobility to the private sector would have been increased. As it was, lack of low cost housing effectively tied much of labor to its current rent-controlled locations.[11] Similarly, if funds had been saved from salaries and invested in infrastructure, the cost of investment to private entrepreneurs would have been lowered, presumably inducing economic growth. Since federal government expenditure comprised

[10] Although alternative employment opportunities exist for skilled workers, there does not appear to be a serious shortage of unskilled workers in the private sector of the economy.

[11] Argentina has recently obtained a $30 million loan from the inter-American Development Banks for housing. Although it has been suggested that the various meat and by-products firms whose plants are located in the *villas miserias* devote part of their profits to housing, this suggestion apparently has been rejected. In addition, electric power plants are located nearby. As a result a number of the most important installations in the economy are located in the midst of some of the most dissatisfied workers. The occupation of these installations by the armed forces gives rise to the disquieting possibility of direct clashes between the military and the Perónists.

almost one fifth of the gross national product, this misallocation was particularly damaging. Ultimately, disguised unemployment in the bureaucracy and armed forces will be overcome only when the private sector can offer enough attractive jobs.

In 1961 as in previous years Argentina depended heavily on imports to supply industrial raw materials, and a shortfall in exchange receipts was to be expected, leading in turn to reduced imports, a cutback in production, and more unemployment. The foreign exchange bottleneck continues. At least one half of anticipated foreign exchange earnings through 1965 are pledged. Of this sum, two thirds represents debts of the national government, state enterprises and the central bank; one third represents private commitments on machinery imported in 1960–1961.

How can more exchange be obtained? The devaluations of 1955 and 1958 lead to an increase of only $15 million in export earnings after each devaluation. So devaluation is an inappropriate method. An alternate method of increasing foreign exchange is the expansion and *diversification* of exports. In 1961, the government was doing relatively little about this crucial problem; Argentina continued to depend on agriculture to supply two thirds of its foreign exchange from export earnings; changeable weather and declining foreign markets made it impossible to predict or to be optimistic about foreign exchange in any given year. On top of this the government varied export retentions and sales taxes not only from year to year but from season to season.

From time to time the government announced policies designed to encourage non-traditional exports, as Dr. Prebisch had recommended, but not much was actually done.[12] It had no clear-cut policy on new investments with high foreign exchange requirements. It let the auto industry drain its reserves until late 1961, and then plugged only part of the leak. No comprehensive system of priorities for the use of foreign exchange was set up, and the various partial systems were ill-enforced.[13] Since the government was not succeeding in pulling Argentina up by its bootstraps, it had

[12] The absence of a well publicized campaign to export woolen textiles or finished leather goods was striking.

[13] A certain amount of opposition to planning stemmed from political opposition to "statism" or to controls reminiscent of the Perón Administration and appeared to be compounded by the belief that Argentina was a developed country to which controls would have been almost humiliatingly inappropriate. Compare page 140 below.

to attract foreign investment or loans. These depended not only on the profitability of individual Argentine firms, but also on the overall economic outlook for the country, on the prospects for continued economic stability, and ultimately on the stability of Frondizi's government.

Thus Argentine economic prospects were clouded even during the relatively favorable early months of 1961. In fact, the ensuing year was marked by a drought that diminished agricultural exports, by a serious railway strike ending in heavy inflationary government expenditure, and by Perónist electoral victories that would have frightened foreign investors even if the military had not then started a new series of coups. Foreign exchange reserves had declined from $705 million in March 1961 to only $351 million in March 1962. A government deficit of 30-40 billion pesos was already anticipated for the fiscal year ending in October 1962. A sharp increase in government revenue and considerable foreign aid would have been necessary to avoid cutbacks in production even if Frondizi had remained in office. Back in 1956, Dr. Prebisch had hoped that the Argentine economy would grow by 40 per cent by 1962; it grew by only 8 per cent.[14]

Eventually one must ask why Argentina's governments *didn't* recast their expenditures and reshape the economy. The answer, of course, is that Argentina belongs to that large majority of countries in which politics help determine the economy. This is not the place to retell Argentine history. But it is obvious that the military factions of Argentina, suspicious of each other and of the other components of society, will neither dissolve themselves nor let a civilian government dismantle them merely because some economists say the money saved might renovate the country. It would be odd if Argentina's defensive rural landowners threw their full energies into building up the industrial sector of the economy, thereby reducing their own power and importance.[15] It would be very odd if Argentine businessmen were eager to give up their privileges and subsidies, or if the Argentine civil service begged to be dismissed from its jobs. After austerity programs and devaluations that bore hardest

[14] Naciones Unidas, *Análisis y proyecciones del desarrollo económico. V. El desarrollo económico de la Argentina,* 1959; and *The Review of the River Plate,* December 31, 1962, p. 495.

[15] See also Aldo Ferrer, "Los problemas de la transición: el caso argentino," in *El Trimestro Económico,* vol. XXX (1), México, Enero–Marzo de 1963, Num. 117.

on the workers, after economy moves that usually forced workers out of their jobs, after agreements with the President that his ministers somehow didn't seem to keep, after the police and the military had been turned loose on strikers, it would stagger belief if the Argentine workers trusted their governments enough to consent to all the government's proposed short-term blows to the workers' position in return for promises that all would be gained back when the national economy, at some future date, took a decisive upturn.

And in so divided and suspicious a society, it is not surprising that political parties do not seriously try to form majority coalitions, but rather split into irreconcilable halves, like the Radical Party. In so emotional an atmosphere, it is not surprising that apparently remote foreign issues, such as whether or not Argentina should vote for the expulsion of Cuba from the O.A.S., have embittering and disruptive effects.

Frondizi was elected with a majority in Congress, essentially because the Perónist workers supported him to show their hostility to the preceding junta and its favorite parties. Frondizi lost the support of most of the Perónist workers, and presently his majority in Congress, largely because of the measures he *did* take to rationalize the economy. He lost what confidence the military and the conservatives had ever had in him by the measures he took to conciliate the workers (handing the Perónist unions back to their Perónist leaders, allowing the Perónists to organize as a party, etc.). He began from a position of relative weakness and lost the strength he had through compromises and waverings. The military juntas that had the power to reshape the economy had neither the knowledge nor the will. The civilian government that *might* have recast the economy simply didn't have the power.

And so Argentina's economy grew by only 8 per cent in almost seven years. And so constitutional government was again overthrown. Familiar "emergency" economic programs were undertaken immediately (e.g., another depreciation), but capital flight, currency depreciation, and domestic inflation persisted. It was estimated that per capita income would decline as much as 10 *per cent* by the end of 1962, and it may well have done so. In November, economy minister Alsogaray announced that the April devaluation and its consequences had increased agricultural producers' income by 72 per cent and decreased workers' income by 15 per cent! The timing and perhaps the depth of the 1962 recession were determined by the putsch, but it should now be clear that 1962 would in any event have been a very troubled year.

VI

One can now judge the three views of Argentina's economic difficulties mentioned at the beginning of this article.

The traditional economic liberals have part of a case. Perón's legacy of state giantism, artificial financial manipulations, and mass featherbedding for political purposes needed to be disposed of. Many clearly necessary steps were taken by successive Argentine governments to free the private sector of the economy and rationalize the state sector. But pure laissez faire is surely not the whole answer. Economically, this is best shown by the recent history of the Argentine auto industry, which, when left to itself, distorted the country's investment into a relatively unproductive set of enterprises. Politically, no democratic Argentine government could impose the sacrifices of a full laissez-faire program on the articulate and organized workers — and no military government has wanted to risk trying.

The Perónists and other radicals have part of a case. "Sellout of the capitalists" is too crude a phrase for the government's complex economic policies, but the net result of the events since 1955 has been to reduce the workers' absolute standard of living, and to reduce their relative share of wealth and power dramatically. Perón increased labor's share of national income from 47 per cent of national income in 1945 to 61 per cent in 1954. Perón's successors reduced the workers' share in national income to 51 per cent in 1959, and it is likely that the share of national income going to workers has continued to decline, in the course of the continuing inflation.

But pure Perónist protection of every wage level and every job of every worker is surely not the whole answer. Economically, this is best shown by the recent history of the Argentine railroads, on which the workers *have*, by and large, maintained their privileged and often unproductive positions, to the demonstrable detriment of the rest of the nation. Politically, the result of serious efforts to conciliate the Perónists is best exemplified by President Frondizi, who is now in a military prison on a small, uncomfortable island.

Nor have the nonpartisan economists resolved all questions. For example, Dr. Prebisch's fund of valuable ideas and the surprising extent to which his advice has been followed have been discussed. Should one say that Argentina's remaining problems come from failure to take the rest of his advice? In part, yes, but in part, this begs the question, for Dr. Prebisch's most basic suggestions were accompanied by his appeal for restraint by all social groups until his reforms could take beneficent effects for all — but the core of Argentina's predicament is precisely the absence of such mutual trust and mutual restraint. It was the social jungle that had led to Perón in the first place!

Perhaps everything will somehow improve of itself, but it looks rather more as if the Argentine political and social deadlock will have to be broken before its economic stagnation can be ended. It is easy to say that a strong government with true authority might reshape the economy to reduce Argentina's dependence on foreign exchange and foreign confidence. It is easy to urge the government to direct investment through requirements on investment of bank portfolios, to give incentives to private industry to invest in desired sectors and locations, to found special credit facilities to aid exports, to invest in infrastructure designed to aid exports, and to pursue all reasonable policies of import substitution. In short, it is easy to tell the Argentines to repeat the rest of the Mexican experience of the last four decades. But how are they to constitute such a strong, wise government? The Argentines have had a charismatic dictator of the "left"; he failed. They are not likely to agree to have a Mexican-style revolution. Yet there is something persuasive in the statement of the Argentine economist, Leopoldo Portnoy:[16]

It will be impossible to develop the country without carrying out profound structural changes. Although it sounds paradoxical, in order to develop the country it is necessary to transform it. This is not the function of economists, but a task reserved to the masses.

---

[16] La realidad argentina en el siglo XX. II. *Análisis Crítico de la Economia, Fondo de Cultura Económica*, 1961, pp. 197–8.

SUGGESTIONS FOR READING

Among studies of revolution as a precondition of economic development are Bert F. Hoselitz, "Nationalism, Economic Development, and Democracy," in Hoselitz, ed., *Agrarian Societies in Transition* (The Annals of the American Academy of Political and Social Science, May, 1956); Robert N. Burr, ed., *Latin America's Nationalistic Revolutions,* The Annals of the American Academy of Political and Social Science (March, 1961); Eugene Staley, *The Future of Underdeveloped Countries: Political Implications of Economic Development* (New York, 1954); and Kalman Silvert's forthcoming book on nationalism and economic development in Latin America.

On the need for land reform or revolution as the key to economic development, see A. I. Tannous, "Land Reform: Key to Development and Stability of the Arab World," *Middle East Journal* (Winter, 1951); United Nations Department of Economic Affairs, *Land Reform: Defects in Agrarian Structure as Obstacles to Economic Development* (New York, 1951); D. Warriner, *Land and Poverty in the Middle East* (London, 1948); D. Warriner, "Land Reform in Egypt and Its Repercussions," *International Affairs* (January, 1953); S. Marii, "The Agrarian Reform in Egypt," *International Labour Review* (February, 1954); and D. Warriner, *Land Reform and Development in the Middle East: A Study of Egypt, Syria and Iraq* (London, 1957).

Social and political concomitants of economic development are discussed in D. H. Buchanan, "Differential Economic Progress: Some Cases, Comparisons, and Contrasts: Japan Versus 'Asia,'" *American Economic Review* (May, 1951); G. I. Blanksten, "Technical Assistance and the Political Instability of Latin America," *Economic Development and Cultural Change,* vol. II, #5 (June, 1954); C. Wolf, "Institutions and Economic Development," *American Economic Review* (December, 1955); E. E. Hagen, "The Process of Economic Development," *Economic Development and Cultural Change,* vol. V, #3 (April, 1957); D. R. Gadgil, "Pre-conditions of Economic Development," *Indian Economic Review* (February, 1952); M. Bronfenbrenner, "The High Cost of Economic Development," *Land Economics* (May, 1953; and P. de Briey, "Industrialisation and Social Problems in Central Africa," *International Labour Review* (May, 1951).

More detailed discussions of the process of economic development are contained in Albert O. Hirschman, *The Strategy of Economic Devel-*

opment (New Haven, 1958); Hirschman, ed., *Latin American Issues, Essays, and Comments* (New York, 1961); P. N. Rosenstein-Rodan, "Problems of Industrialization of Eastern and South-Eastern Europe," *Economic Journal* (June-September, 1943); Y. L. Wu, "A Note in the Post-War Industrialization of 'Backward' Countries and Centralist Planning," *Economica* (August, 1945); United Nations Technical Assistance Administration, *Report of the United Nations Economic Mission to Chile, 1949–1950* (New York, 1951); and H. W. Spiegel, *The Brazilian Economy: Chronic Inflation and Sporadic Industrialization* (Philadelphia, 1949).

More detailed studies of the role of planning in economic development are B. V. N. Naidu, "Planning in Underdeveloped Countries," *Indian Economic Journal* (July, 1953); Political and Economic Planning, "The Strategy of World Development," *Planning*, 23 (April, 1951); United Nations, *Manual on Economic Development Projects* (New York, 1958); and United Nations Economic Commission for Latin America, *Economic Development, Planning and International Cooperation* (Santiago, 1961).

A striking case study of the achievements possible following a revolution is available in three books by Frank Tannenbaum: *The Mexican Agrarian Revolution* (New York, 1929); *Mexico, The Struggle for Peace and Bread* (New York, 1950); and *Peace by Revolution* (New York, 1933). Detailed background on pre-revolutionary Bolivia is presented in *Report of the United Nations Technical Assistance Mission to Bolivia* (New York, 1951). An attempt to bring the story of the Bolivian revolution up to date is given by Robert J. Alexander, *The Bolivian National Revolution* (Rutgers, 1958). A more detailed statement of Celso Furtado's views is in *The Economic Growth of Brazil* (University of California, 1963); additional studies of Brazil are S. Kuznets, W. E. Moore, and J. J. Spengler, eds., *Economic Growth: Brazil, India, Japan* (Durham, N. C., 1955), and Spiegel, *op cit.* The best known statement of Dr. Predisch's views is presented in United Nations Economic Commission for Latin America, *The Economic Development of Latin America and Its Principal Problems* (New York, 1950).

Other studies of interest are H. S. Ellis, ed., *Economic Development for Latin America* (New York, 1961); H. G. Aubrey, "The Role of the State in Economic Development," *American Economic Review* (May, 1951); B. F. Hoselitz, ed., *The Progress of Underdeveloped Areas* (Chicago, 1952); and G. A. Almond and J. S. Coleman, eds., *The Politics of the Developing Areas* (Princeton, 1960).